This book is dedicated to my Grandfather Alexander Keith, who sold office supplies in Toronto, Ontario, Canada. He went door to door to various offices in the early 1900s. He made his calls by riding the streetcar and carrying his product samples in a briefcase. Thank you Grandpa, you're still the best Salesperson I know. Thanks for the Legacy.

Love, Bruce

To Bill

Keep growing your Data Base.

[illegible]

ACKNOWLEDGMENT

Special thanks to Cathy Kozma for her amazing proofreading skills. Her tireless efforts in correcting all my literary gaffes is much appreciated. Her desire for everything to be "just perfect" is admirable! Cathy herself is a very accomplished Salesperson and was the perfect choice to bring everything to final copy. She "gets it". Thank you Cathy... you set a terrific example. BK

PREFACE

Spending in excess of 40 continuous years in sales is bound to create some "inside knowledge". Starting with calling on car repair shops for a fledgling rent-a-car business, to selling Memory Typewriters (that's what they were called before PCs) for IBM Canada Ltd., to doorknocking in the real estate business, to Coaching thousands of Salespeople in various lines of commissioned sales makes for a lot of rejection, a lot of success... and most of all, a lot of valuable lessons.

You don't start out selling newspapers for the London Free Press at the age of 8 and say to yourself *"I'm going to be selling for the rest of my life"*. You don't knock on doors in your neighborhood as a child offering to cut grass for 75 cents per hour and say to yourself *"Guess what Bruce... you're going to be doorknocking for the rest of your life"*. But that's what ended up happening ... and, in looking back, I guess it was always destined to be. The process of selling is pretty straightforward. Take a product that you believe in, develop an approach to help people see the benefits, take a deep breath, and jump into the Sales Game.

The passion was always there. Sometimes you don't know this until you look back. What comes with the passion and the 40+ years in business is an incredible amount of experience that has helped me improve every day. This book is a compilation of some of the wisdom I have learned through "stubbing my toe" over and over, plus the exhilaration of accumulative successes. It's also packed with Action Steps ... real, "no nonsense" strategies that you can use to take your business to the NEXT! level. The Business of Sales is not easy but it is tremendously rewarding, both financially and emotionally. Enjoy these tips and these vignettes and build your Sales Career to new heights every day! It's all about believing in yourself, it's all about growth, it's all about becoming the person you know is inside you. Enjoy the journey. **NO Excuses.**

Bruce Keith

NEXT!...

Powerful Sales Strategies

Volume II

101 Results-Based Sales Strategies
For Sales Professionals

TABLE OF CONTENTS

Chapter 1
Creating & Closing Sales

Free at Last!

GET OUT of JAIL... The problem with the "Sales Game" is that some of the customers don't treat us with respect. They are not pleasant to work with... no matter how hard we try. The good news about the "Sales Game" is that we DO NOT have to work with anyone we don't want to! If they do not treat us with the same respect that we show them ... get rid of them!

Here is your **ACTION STEP ...** first of all, ask yourself the "Acid Test" question ... *"How does that customer make me feel about myself?"* If the answer is *"Not so good"* then you have two choices:

1. *Refer them out to someone else and get a referral fee ... or,*

2. *Just say "I'm afraid I can't help you" and turn them loose.*

NOTE: There is no 3rd choice here ... if they make you feel badly about yourself then it is like sitting beside a sick person on an airplane. **Sooner or later they will infect you!** Stay healthy. Stay free. Cut them loose and you will feel like you "just got out of jail"!! Now, go out and find somebody who appreciates your skills and talents. There are plenty of them out there. **NO Excuses.**

Where's My Boots?

GET YOUR BOOTS READY... If you were to tour your local firehall you'd see all the equipment lined up beside the truck ... nice and neat and ready to go. Boots, hats, coats, etc. WHY? So that when the bell goes off we don't have a bunch of guys and girls running around screaming, *"Have you seen my boots?"!!!*

Here is your **ACTION STEP ...** first of all ask, *"Where are my boots?"* Do you come in to work and waste Prime-Time looking for your boots? Or are they already lined up beside the truck? Let me be more specific...

Your BOOTS are the people you need to call in the AM to drive your business ... your prospecting phone #s. If I came to your office first thing in the AM, where would I find your boots? Would they be in a neat pile in plain sight or would they be scattered over the place?

Remember the affirmation *"My day begins the night before"*. Get all your prospecting #s ready before you go home. Stop sabotaging your mornings! By doing it the night before, you'll be way more productive and you can get started prospecting on time ... just like it says in your daily schedule. **NO Excuses.**

Warmer or Colder?

EASTER EGG HUNT… Remember as a child when you used to hunt for eggs at Easter? All the children would run around squealing wildly while they were searching for treasures. The parents would give guidance by saying either *"You're getting warmer"* or *"You're getting colder"*. The temperature analogy was designed to tell the children if they were getting closer to the goal or further away. The Selling Business is much like an Easter Egg Hunt. How so?

Here is your **ACTION STEP…** life's little lessons never seem to change. The treasures you are looking for are no longer Easter Eggs. **The desired target is now new Sales Leads**…but you still have to go out looking for them, don't you? How does all this apply to Sales? Here is the game now:

1. *Ask yourself… what Easter Eggs am I looking for today? (What do I want to find? Be specific…new opportunities, appointments, etc.)*

2. *Start looking early in the day (Lead generation should always be in the morning)*

3. *Be your own thermometer. (Ask, with this new lead… am I getting warmer? or… am I getting colder?)*

4. *Be honest with yourself. (Am I spending enough time looking for "Easter Eggs"? & Am I looking in the right places?)*

Start today with a very focused Easter Egg Hunt, and don't get off track! The equation is simple, more eggs = more money. **NO Excuses.**

Milk or Veggies?

MILKMAN OR GREENGROCER?... We all love stories. Great Salespeople use stories to help illustrate a point with their customers. A friend recently shared a fascinating insight. He told me that when he was a youngster growing up in Holland, *"the retail business was much different"*. The Milkman would knock on every door and ask the occupants if they wanted any milk that day. There was also a "Greengrocer" who toured the streets selling vegetables from his truck. The difference was that the Greengrocer would stay in his truck, ring the bell, and wait for buyers to come to him, while the Milkman went door to door. Two different approaches.

Here is your **ACTION STEP...** this is a great metaphor and here is the real message. **Both the Milkman AND the Greengrocer thought they were in the Selling business.** The truth is... only one was Selling. The other was merely an Order Taker!

1. *Which one do you suppose made more Sales?*
2. *Which one are you??*

Great Salespeople always ASK for business... they DO NOT wait for the Customer to come to them. What do you do? Are you the Milkman or the Greengrocer? Be sure you're not guilty of seducing yourself into thinking that you are asking for business when you are not! Sure, Selling involves some risk, but don't you deserve the rewards? Don't wait in the truck. **NO Excuses.**

What do you believe?

THE BELIEF TRANSFER... Everyone has a series of beliefs. These beliefs dictate how we operate on a day-to-day basis. We believe that if we eat properly we will be healthier. We believe that if we work hard we will get results. We believe that if we behave ethically we will be rewarded. Typically our beliefs are based on what we have been taught and/or what we have experienced. Most of the time we are right... but not always. Read on.

In Sales we frequently draw on our beliefs to decide what we're going to do and what we are going to say. The trouble is ... sometimes our beliefs are ill-founded and we mistakenly believe that "everyone else feels the same way". **We assume that everyone believes what we believe.** Critical Point: sometimes they don't! This concept of "everyone feeling the same way" can be **described as a Belief Transfer.**

Here is your **ACTION STEP...** if a particular belief of ours is incorrect and we "Belief Transfer" then we are limiting our chances of success. Here are some examples of Incorrect Belief Transfers. **It is incorrect to believe that:**

1. *If I close five times I will irritate my customers. (For some yes, but they are a very small minority and probably aren't motivated anyway)*

2. *If I ask direct questions, my customers will think I am "pushy". (Example: "Are you ready to sign the agreement?")*

3. *If I use a script, my customers will "catch me doing so" and find me unprofessional. (A well-practiced*

conversation is much more professional than winging it)

4. *If I follow up on my leads "sooner than later" my customers will be turned off. (You will lose much more business by following up too late than you will by following up too soon!)*

Have a look at the situations where you are guilty of a Belief Transfer that is invalid. Let's say that you are looking at a proven Sales Conversation. If you find yourself saying, *"If someone said that to me I would hang up on them"* then your Belief Transfer is holding you back. This is one of those "get out of the box" scenarios... that particular script has been used with great results hundreds and hundreds of times already. Be brutally honest with yourself and look for areas that you can become more versatile. Growth is always good. **NO Excuses.**

Lottery Ticket Security

I'LL CHECK LATER... The other day while paying for some gasoline I was delayed while some poor soul ahead of me in line spent $91.00 on lottery tickets! That in itself was a bit depressing. Here was this guy spending all that money on a pipe dream, over which he had absolutely no control. So I asked him, *"Are you winning or losing?"* His response was that he was *"doing okay"*. Then he gave me the shocker... he said, *"Sometimes I don't check my tickets for weeks on end"*. I thought about this as I drove away and then I realized there is a Sales Tip here.

Here is your **ACTION STEP...** the reason he wasn't checking his lottery tickets weekly was to help "keep his dream alive". As long as he didn't know that "he had not won... then he didn't know **that he had lost!**" Don't we do that sometimes as Salespeople with our leads? Don't we hang onto our leads like they are lottery tickets? That way we'll never know the rejection... in case they say no. We avoid calling them. We protect ourselves. Here's a better approach:

1. *Call ALL your leads a minimum of once a week*
2. *Find out if you have a "winning ticket" sooner... not later*
3. *If it's a "losing ticket"... throw it away*
4. *It's better to have no leads than a bunch of "losers"*
5. *Go out and "buy" some new tickets every day (meaning, prospect daily!)*

The good news is that the Selling Game is not a lottery. You can always get more winning tickets just by talking to more people and asking for business. Always "check your tickets" right away. Find out quick and move on. **NO Excuses.**

Earning Referrals

REFERRALS ARE LIKE OXYGEN... they are the lifeblood of any great Sales business. We need to ask these questions over and over, every day... *"Who do you know who needs my help to buy or sell a home in the next 90 days?". Or "Who do you know who needs my help to invest in my product this year?". Or "Who do you know who you could send my way, and who I should speak to right now?"*. Before you can ask those questions, the first thing you must do is **build up a sizeable Database** of people who will refer their friends and relatives.

Reality Check: every business starts with a zero Database. The size of your Database is purely a function of how many people that you contact on an ongoing basis. **The results you receive from that Database are directly related to the quality of your service.** The key then is to garner a high percentage of referrals from your Database.

Here is your **ACTION STEP...** the way to get a lot of referrals from your Database is to get people to talk about you. What is it about you that makes it easy for people to send business your way? **It must be easy for them to explain why you are better to do business with.** For example:

- *"Fred is great to do business with, he is always there when you need him and treats you like you are his only customer."*

- *"I would recommend Judy to anyone. She really knows the market, works very hard and doesn't waste any of my time. She's very efficient!"*

- *"We clicked right away with Susan. She asked all the right questions and knew immediately what we were looking for. She then went out and got it for us. She listens."*

- *"John has some very unique ways of getting results. His marketing and follow-up campaigns are second to none. I've never met anyone who does things as uniquely as he does. He is simply a great Salesperson"*

The 4 examples above are real life referral stories I collected from some of my Coaching clients. Their customers found it *"easy to explain why they are superior to the competition"*. Make sure your customers can do the same about you. **Bonus Tip:** start asking your customers what it is about you that they like. Look for commonalities that allow you to focus on the specific things that are working for you. Build on your strengths. Stand out! **NO Excuses!**

Tips for Working Smart!

"HOW'S IT GOING?"... is a very common question that all Salespeople need to answer on an ongoing basis. People always ask us that. Our typical answer is... *"It's Going Great! I'm Really Busy!"*. That's a pretty standard response and it really doesn't say much. The truth is that most of the people who are asking you that question don't want a detailed answer anyway. My question for you is... ***Are you "really busy" doing Busy Work or are you really busy working on your Hot Leads?*** What are you working on? Busy Work or Hot Leads?

Here is your **ACTION PLAN...** too often we become "seduced" by how hard we're working and forget the purpose of the exercise... i.e.: to create Sales volume this month. There are **two major components to Success in Sales:**

Component #1. You have to work hard every day (no surprises here!)

Component #2. Your Hard Work must be focused on your Hot Leads List

Once you have decided to do #1, then you can go to #2. Here's how:

1. *Make a short list of your Hot Leads (those prepared to do business in the next 30 days)*
2. *Keep this list with you at all times... and be honest in answering, "Is my list long enough to meet my goals?" (This is a critical question, and if not... see #5 below)*

3. *Make sure there is a specific Follow-Up Date written down for each prospect*

4. *Call them on the day you said you were going to... no procrastination allowed*

5. *If your list is too short... set aside 2 hours every day to find additions, because there are people out there who need you!*

This process needs to be repeated over and over. Commit to being more than “I’m really busy”. **Commit to being busy with great Prospects... your Hot Leads.** Avoid being one of those who works hard 12 months a year and has very little to show for it. The alternative is yours for the asking! **NO Excuses.**

How do They do That?

COMMON PERFECTION... What do the following top performers have in common ... a Broadway Actor, an MVP Baseball Player and a Great Salesperson?

Answer... they all have mastered the Power of Routine. The Broadway Actor performs the same lines and the same actions every night. The audience never considers that they are witnessing a Routine. A great Baseball Player goes through the same motions and series of habits every time he steps up to the plate. Great Salespeople do the same things: a) over and over, b) at the same time of day, c) in the same way. There is no variation in the way they perform their tasks... sure, they are very good at what they do but... the real power comes from their **ability to do seemingly boring tasks at the top of the scale, every time**! This is how you capitalize on the Power of Routine.

Here is your **ACTION STEP...** let's look at why a Routine works so well...

1. *You start by developing a system*
2. *You create a series of habits (i.e.: a Routine)*
3. *It gets easier every time you do it*
4. *You now have huge confidence in your ability because "it works every time!"*
5. *It is now natural to do the same thing, the same way, over and over*

Homework: start by looking at some of your day-to-day activities and see how strong your Routine is (examples: your morning routine, your practicing routine, your presentation routine). Remember that following a Routine is not a signal for boredom to take over. **The benefit of doing things the same way is that it creates predictability in the outcome.** You do not have to forfeit your spontaneity or your enthusiasm for the task at hand. Have fun, be energetic, and never let your "audience" sense that you are doing something that is very repetitive for you. As Jim Carey said in "The Mask"... It's Showtime! **NO Excuses.**

Where's That Lead?

HOT PINK... ever get a great lead and then misplace it? Worse still, ever get a great lead and then forget about it until it shows up as a Sale under someone else's name?!! In spite of our advancing technology there are two common problems for Salespeople when it comes to Lead Management:

1. "Bruce, if I put it in my computer, I run the risk of losing it... out of sight, out of mind"
2. "If I put it on paper, it'll get lost in the shuffle!"

Here is your **ACTION STEP...**

1. *The only leads you should put on paper are the HOT, HOT, 30 day leads*
2. *Put the longer leads in your computer with a "reminder flag" for follow up*
3. *Create a standard "LEAD FOLLOW UP" form (Don't forget to include the some space for your "follow up" instructions to yourself)*
4. *Take the form to a copy shop and get them to produce 50 Lead Follow Up pages on HOT PINK paper*
5. *Put only your best leads on these pages*

The HOT PINK is reserved ONLY for your special 30 day leads... they will light up your desk and **you will never lose them**. It's magic! **NO Excuses.**

I Don't Wanna

NOT TODAY... one of the Rules of Success is to consistently do the things that unsuccessful people do not want to do. At the top of this list is the dreaded **Lead Generation, Prospecting, Profit Seeking Time** (or whatever you want to call it). 99% of Salespeople do not like to prospect. Why would you?... It's boring, it's hard work, and you're sure to get lots of rejection. The other side of that of course is: 1) there are lots of methods of Lead Generation and more importantly... 2) that's what starts the Sales Cycle. That's how you get paid the "big bucks"!

Here is your **ACTION STEP...** not only does Prospecting start the Sales Cycle but it's really what decides your income in the long run.

If you are resisting the process of creating new leads here is a simple approach designed to help you be more consistent:

1. *Write out all the reasons you do not like to Lead Generate/Prospect*

2. *Cross out the ones that are based on whining* (remember, you are in the Sales Game... whining doesn't pay much)

3. *Look at the ones that are left and ask yourself this question, "Is the pain of prospecting greater than the pain of not succeeding???"*

4. *CRITICAL POINT... last question to ask yourself, "What is my alternative?"*

If the answer is... *"Start a new career"*, then go and do it. If the answer is... *"This is my best option"*, then start

Prospecting! Put in your schedule (preferably in the morning), get someone to hold you accountable, and get on with being a Great Salesperson. Have a great life!... you deserve it and it's there for the asking. **NO Excuses.**

Chapter 2
Better Time Management

Where's Your Schedule?

DAILY SCHEDULE... great salespeople have a daily routine, and they have a set Schedule.

Everyone knows this and it's tough to follow it every day. The key is to keep it simple and only do one thing at a time - the item that is designated for that time of day. Salespeople who "wing it" are always in react mode. They never "have enough time" to get things done. They end up playing that game the kids play at the fall fair... they play "whack-a-mole"!

Here is your **ACTION STEP...** create a 5 Days a Week Schedule...

1. *Remember "the AM is for lead generation & the PM is for lead servicing",*
2. *ONLY schedule the "must do" items in your routine, (lead generation, follow-up, appointments, etc.)*
3. *Eliminate the temptations that can interrupt you*
4. *Get really good at saying NO when your routine is threatened*
5. *Type it out and POST IT EVERYWHERE.*

Be committed to using a daily schedule... there's huge money in following a routine. The alternative is just another excuse for underachieving. **NO Excuses.**

Dangers of Multi-Tasking

MULTI-TASKING... every day the danger of "getting off-track" rears its ugly head and we have to deal with it. Most Salespeople fall into the *"Black Hole of Multi-Tasking"*, or trying to do more than one thing at a time. Let's be very clear here... **Multi-Tasking is NOT AN ASSET!!!** Studies have shown that trying to do more than one thing at a time will reduce your efficiency by as much as 80%... YES, that's 80%!! Also, what's worse is that the task that suffers most is always the most important one of the group. The brain is programmed to always default to the easiest task.

Here is your **ACTION STEP...**

1. *Sop patting yourself on the back for thinking you are really good at doing more than one thing at a time;*

2. *Commit to doing exactly what your daily schedule says you are to do right now;*

3. *When another item needing your attention appears take 30 seconds (maximum) & write it down as a reminder for later;*

4. *DO NOT let other people's emergencies become your problems... use your self-discipline and do things on your time, not theirs.*

Do these 4 steps and you will always win! Do not and you'll always have a long list of excuses. Remember... **NO Excuses.**

I am So Busy

BUSY WORK... ever get through the day, take a deep breath, and say to yourself: *"Whew... now that was a busy day!"?* We all have and it feels good, doesn't it? Not so fast Superstar... the real question is the next one: *"Did you get anything done that was important?"*

Here is your **ACTION STEP...** we all know people who specialize in Busy Work. To make sure you are not one of those, here are some steps to follow:

1. *Do your usual "to do" list before the day starts,*
2. *Critical Step... remind yourself: My job today is to* ***sell something,***
3. *Re-do your list so that the "sell something" items always Come First,*
4. *NOW, go"sell something". Ask yourself this question... "Who can I talk to today who will help me make money this week?"*

Keep holding yourself accountable to this 4 step formula. Repeat this Affirmation, with enthusiasm: *"Busy work has disappeared from my life... Yes!"* **NO Excuses.**

...Oops!

PROGRESS HAS CREATED A PROBLEM... the Internet has changed the Business World. For that matter, the Internet has changed the whole world, not just Business. Everything is faster, everything is more accessible, everything is right at our fingertips. The world has gotten smaller. As author Thomas Freidman explained in his bestseller, ***The World Is Flat,*** the new generation of Salespeople (plus we 'older' ones, who have converted) are operating our businesses completely differently. For the most part the "operating differently" approach is better. There is one hidden problem however... **the Internet sabotages Sustained Attention!** Because everything is so readily accessible, many Salespeople operate 100% in React Mode. When that happens, Sustained Attention to a particular task or focus point can erode quickly. To always be in a state of Reaction **prevents planned growth and often prevents daily progress.**

Here is your **ACTION STEP...** here are the problems that being too attached to the Internet (and your cell phone) can create:

1. **Sustained attention disappears**... single tasks do not get completed in a timely fashion

2. The desire for **instant gratification can get in the way** of meaningful activities

3. **Multitasking becomes a point of pride**... make no mistake, the mind is not equipped to do more

than one task at a time! The experts all agree on this point, and the result is built-in inefficiency

But wait... let's not get in the way of progress! Is there a solution? Of course. there is; here are two very clear answers...

1. *Have a **solid routine** to follow that allows uninterrupted "time blocking" for the most important tasks of your day. This is especially true for your morning.*

2. *Get very good at **saying NO** to interruptions and short-term items that creep into your mind and your day. This is a "learned skill". It takes practice, but anyone can do it. The most efficient Salespeople are masters at "saying NO".*

This Sales Tip is not about "dissing" the Internet. It is about understanding the inherent pitfalls of "sabotaging Sustained Attention". **The idea of doing one thing at a time is pretty basic.** It has not changed with technology. The ability to focus and concentrate on the most important items in your business and your life are critical. Every time you find your mind wandering to another task make the decision to finish what you are doing before you start the next item.

Bonus Point: one of the best ways to do this is to eliminate the temptation. When you are doing something really important, turn off your cell phone and your e-mail. What you don't know won't hurt you (or anyone else for that matter) for the next 1 to 2 hours.

Everything will carry on quite well without you for a short period. **NO Excuses.**

Sales Killer #6

NO, NO, NO... Sales Killer #6 is **not being able to say NO!** Years ago, First Lady Nancy Reagan launched a "No Drugs" campaign with the slogan... *Just Say NO!* I don't know how successful that program was but I do know that it is a great mantra to use in the Sales game. Perhaps it should be rephrased to read... *"Just **Learn** to Say NO!".* Many times I get calls for Help Me! from Salespeople who do not know how to turn away prospects who are 1) not motivated or 2) not qualified or 3) unrealistic. Those leads are *"time vampires".* They always add up to a recipe for frustration and no results.

Here is your **ACTION PLAN...** the next three steps are simple (but I didn't say they were easy)

1. *Remind yourself every day of your BIG purpose (your priority is to earn $$$, not to babysit "fence sitting" Clients)*

2. *Identify the actions needed to do that (usually it is to find people who really need you, and then help them)*

3. *If they do not pass step #2, tell them "I'm afraid I can't help you" and move on!*

Bonus Point... and this is the 'toughie'. If you're already working with a *"time vampire"* be strong enough to admit it and use step #3 on them too... fast! Stop telling yourself that *"I've got so much time invested in them, I can't afford to let them go".* Top producers move fast and replace those leads immediately. Just Say NO! **NO Excuses.**

Good Growth or Bad Growth?

GROWTH THAT WORKS... everyone grows, every day, and everything we do creates growth. The resulting growth can be good or bad. The key is to make sure that your growth is beneficial. One of the things that grows on an ongoing basis is the amount of potential business we generate. In other words, new leads or opportunities can lead to further success. When we prospect consistently, when we ask for more business, things happen. Even if it is just "over lunch" with another individual, there are always new openings and possibilities for us to pursue. The key is to make sure that we handle the growth wisely.

Here is your **ACTION STEP...** the more people we talk to, the more leads we generate. So far, so good. Here is where you can really shine! Have a plan to manage all the great new activity you have created. As the # of opportunities expand, the next three steps are critical to **"growth that works"**:

1. *Raise the bar... be tougher on who you accept as a lead*

2. *Move faster through the leads you accept, and if they are not ready to act... move on*

3. *Put all your energy into "Now Business"... and follow them up first thing every day*

Bonus Tip: do not get bogged down with leads that are going nowhere or should be placed in a "longer-term follow-up" file. Why? Some Salespeople go through a cycle of *"I have so many leads, I'd better stop prospecting until I can get these ones under control".* Then they stop prospecting. That's not good! The Superstars follow the above three steps on an ongoing basis. The result is a much smoother path of higher quality leads, resulting in more business and more revenue. Most important of all, because you are **focusing on the customers who REALLY need you...** you have a much smoother cash flow. Nice! That's the way you wanted it to be when you started out, right? **NO Excuses.**

Become an Efficiency Expert

TIME LADDER... everyone has challenges periodically with Time Management. The business world we operate in continually assaults even our best attempts to stay on schedule. Only the very highly disciplined Salespeople manage to stay on schedule. Interestingly enough, the very highly disciplined Salespeople earn the most money! Everyone else says things like, *"I just have so much to do, it's not my fault... the day just seem to fly by. It's not like I am not working, you know?"* So how do the Superstars do it?

Here is your **ACTION STEP...** here is a technique that will really take you to the heart of the problem. Efficiency experts use this approach in large corporations. It is called a TIME LADDER. Here's how it works:

1. *Take a blank Daily Planner page and copy it five times. One for Monday, Tuesday, etc.*

2. *For the next week fill in exactly WHAT YOU DID in 15 minute increments.* ***Do this as the day goes on, and <u>not</u> at the end of the day.*** *Do this for one week exactly as instructed... do not cut corners. Do not resist... it's only for a week and...* ***this approach can change your life!***

3. *Now have a look at all the stuff you shouldn't have done (and be brutally honest here) and highlight the non-productive items in bright yellow*

4. *Immediately stop doing the things that are not "revenue producing activities"... stop doing the things you highlighted. Most of all, make sure you definitely protect your mornings! The AM is Prime Time.*

If you really want to become super-efficient, do the above exercise for one week. You will learn a lot and you'll be able to correct your inefficiencies instantaneously. The TIME LADDER is an amazing way to identify where you are "spinning your wheels". Don't do that anymore! **NO Excuses.**

How to Avoid Overkill

CUSTOMER SERVICE or CUSTOMER SMOTHERING?... I came across a great quote the other day in "Success" Magazine. The Publisher, Darren Hardy, was saying that *"Business is about providing customer service to the extent that you make money".* It was one of those statements that seemed so obvious that I had to read it twice to appreciate the wisdom of its simplicity. There are three components to be considered... 1) your business; 2) customer service; & 3) making money. What I found so interesting is that even the best Salespeople lose sight sometimes of the necessity to keep a balance between those three items.

Here is your **ACTION STEP...** my years in the Sales Business have taught me that where Salespeople get off-track is frequently in item #2... the Customer Service component. Most of the time we are not guilty of giving poor service; most of the time we are guilty of GIVING TOO MUCH SERVICE! What we do is we smother, incubate, mother, and generally provide much more service than (a) the customer needs, and more importantly, (b) than the customer wants. To be sure that you are on track, do a quick analysis of your business:

1. *Decide why you are in business... is it to **make a profit** or is it to **gain friends**?*

2. *If it is for **Profit**: look for the times when you are giving more service than is necessary to get the job done properly*

3. *Critical point: Now start using the time you have saved (in #2) to add more people to your "conveyor belt" and create more leads*

4. *Otherwise, if it is to **Gain Friends**: keep over-servicing them and be satisfied with less profitable results.*

Just remember that Great Service is giving your customers what they want. Sometimes when you "over-deliver" you are doing so at the expense of your own profitability. *"Under-promise and over-deliver"* has its limits! Draw the line somewhere in the middle and everybody will be happy. **NO Excuses.**

Creating Momentum Now

HUFFING & PUFFING... recently, in the midst of a marvellous family vacation in Italy, the concept of Creating Momentum appeared to me in a crowded train station. It was a modern day view of *"The Little Engine That Could"*. You know the scene... as the train was ready to leave the station there was a lot of energy spent in getting moving. Even with modern day technology the engine had to strain to move the heavy load it was pulling. There was lots of "huffing and puffing" at the start and not much to show for it, considering the effort expended. The resulting momentum did not come easily, but it did happen. Creating Momentum requires commitment and... initially... extra effort.

Here is your **ACTION STEP...** if you want sustained results you have to be committed. If you are committed you will Create Momentum. **Most people give up too soon.** Here is a simple plan to Create Momentum:

1. *Decide where you want to go (e.g. results, by a certain date)*

2. *Calculate what needs to be achieved each month (e.g. "x" number of sales)*

3. *Focus only on the first month (do not look too far ahead!)*

4. *Establish the activities needed for the first week of that month*

5. *Write out a ROCK-SOLID daily routine to support this*

6. *Go to bed early, set your alarm, and jump out of bed on time!*

7. *Repeat this process day after day and week after week... NO Excuses.*

Creating Momentum can be summed up this way... *"it's usually pretty simple, it's just not very easy".* What's exciting, though, is that while all worthwhile endeavours take some time to get started they are **much harder to stop... once you get going.** The competition ususally just doesn't have the commitment to *"get out of the station"*. Commit today and Create Momentum. **NO Excuses.**

My Priorities

PLAN B – AN OPTION… there's never a day that goes by in my business of doing Seminars and Personal Coaching that the issue of Time Management doesn't come up. Everyone has issues with the fact that there are only 24 hours in each day. One solution is to create a Daily Schedule and stick to it… well, surprise-surprise… that doesn't work for some people! There is another solution.

Here is your **ACTION STEP…** take a different approach (and please read through these next steps more than once… they just may change your life!):

1. *Make a list of the 5-8 things that you must do every day to make your life run properly (such as: prospect, role play, & lead follow up)*

2. *Be sure to include some personal items (including exercise and getting to bed on time)*

3. *Create a simple **DAILY ACCOUNTABILITY CHECKLIST** that lists these tasks, plus columns for each day of the week*

4. *This is NOT a "to do" list… it is a list of your "Things I must do daily to make my life run smoothly"*

5. *Don't worry about what order the tasks are completed. Just make sure you do each of them EVERY DAY*

6. *As each task is completed, put a checkmark in each box for that particular day. Your target is to have checkmarks in 85% of the boxes*

If you can't seem to stick to your Daily Schedule... use the Daily Accountability Checklist. Either way you will be a better Salesperson! **NO Excuses.**

Chapter 3
Powerful Presentations & Objection Handling

Charlie Chaplin

SMILE, SMILE, SMILE.... The great comedian Charlie Chaplin had a Theme Song entitled "Smile" (performed by Nat King Cole). What do we do when we meet someone for the first time? We look them in the eye, give them a firm handshake, and we....SMILE. We always SMILE. No big deal, every great Salesperson does that. Why do we SMILE? Because it helps break the ice, presents us in a positive light, and helps build rapport. It tells people who we are!

Here is your **ACTION STEP...** too often we offer the SMILE initially and then forget about it for the rest of the relationship.

Remember that:

1. *Your SMILE is a very powerful way of communicating*

2. *It sets the tone for every conversation*

3. *People can tell when you are smiling over the phone*

4. *Not smiling makes you less attractive*

5. *You should keep smiling all the time... and why not?*

BONUS TIP: practice smiling all the time, and use it in every contact you have. Test yourself regularly and ask

"Am I smiling right now?". It will make you feel GREAT about YOU, too! **NO Excuses.**

Do You Know?

NO IDEA... customers are always asking us questions. They need information. That's their job, and that's how they make decisions. Our job is to give them as much information as they need so they can say Yes or No. Sometimes when we don't know the answer our EGO gets in the way. What we make the mistake of doing is... we "wing" it, or we guess, or we make up an answer. You know, the sort of things Jim Carrey ("Dumb & Dumber") or Steve Martin ("The Jerk") always do in their classic comedies. Needless to say, they always get in trouble and it backfires. Not so for you...

Here is your **ACTION STEP...** the main reason we get in trouble is that we think the customer expects us to know everything! Well they don't... here's the correct answer:

> *"You know, that's a good question. I am not sure about that so what I'll do is find out and then we'll both be sure. It's my job to get you the correct fact. I'll be glad to get back to you about that in ________, OK?"*

Here's a tip to really do it right... if you're face to face with a customer, write down the question in front of them. It is very reassuring, and it shows that you are listening. If you're on the phone, make sure to say *"Let me make a note of that right now".*

This is what a true professional does. The client will appreciate your honesty. Be sure to get back to them in a timely fashion, and then they know you are your word. Keep winning! **NO Excuses.**

What Attracts People?

TORTISE OR HARE... recently while ascending a very narrow staircase I was struck by how slowly the person in front of me was actually moving. A few minutes later, while walking across a rather busy parking lot, I noticed the same thing with many of my fellow shoppers. They all seem to be following Aesop's suggestion that *"Slow but steady wins the race".* That may be true for children's fables but it sure is a questionable strategy in Sales! One of the more important characteristics in selling is to *"Have a Sense of Urgency in Everything You Do".*

Here is your **ACTION STEP...** having a **Sense of Urgency** doesn't mean running around willy-nilly in circles. It means get on with what you are doing, take action, create results, and move on. Here's what the pros do:

1. *View the task at hand and decide what needs to be done*

2. *Don't think about it once you have decided, just take action*

3. ***Critical Point:** look like you are busy, look like you are intentional, move with energy! Send out the right message.*

4. *On those days you don't feel like it, it's okay...* ***just fake it!...*** *but keep moving!*

Your customers are attracted to Energy. **People Are Attracted to Energy!** Give off that feeling of confidence and productivity. When you're moving fast, things happen, so be one of those who attracts success. **NO Excuses.**

Are you really different?

WHAT'S UNIQUE ABOUT YOU... is what defines the difference between you and your competition. What separates Starbucks from the competition is the high quality of their product and the consistency. That's what makes them unique. There are no surprises when you go there. You know exactly what you're going to get. If you liked their coffee the last time, you will like it this time. **To be a great Salesperson, there must be something about you that is Unique.** One of my Coaching clients who earns approximately $1 million per year, every year, never misses prospecting three hours per day 220 days per year. He is incredibly consistent. That makes him unique. What allows you to stand out in the marketplace? Here is the key... there must be an easy way for your customers to differentiate between you and all the other Salespeople. That's what will make it easy to choose you.

Here is your **ACTION STEP... You need to make sure that your "uniqueness" is highly visible.** Some differences that Salespeople exhibit are highly visible and some are not. Here are some ideas:

1. *Your energy level, your enthusiasm*

2. *Your frequency of contact, you always stay in touch*

3. *The professionalism you portray*

4. *Your work ethic*

5. *Your ability to "get things done", you take action*

6. *Your superb Customer Service*

Whatever your Unique item is, some days it will be harder than others for you to make it highly visible. For example, being extra cheerful on a day you have receive a lot of rejection is not easy. That's where the *"fake it until you make it"* part comes in. Your customers are paying for their "perception" of who you are that day. It doesn't matter to them how you feel inside. Be strong and keep your Uniqueness intact and highly visible. That's what sets you apart. **NO Excuses!**

Do they pay attention?

THE GREAT COMMUNICATOR... it's as simple as this, **if you are a great Communicator then you are a great Salesperson.** The best Salespeople focus on their communication skills because they know this is their "meal ticket" to success.

Here is your **ACTION STEP...** Know the four main components of being a great Communicator:

1. **Sincerity** – *if you believe it then it will be a lot easier for them to believe it. Once you have sold yourself then the rest becomes much more natural.*

2. **Repetition** – *saying the same things, the same way, over and over. Be consistent in your words. That way you get better every time you present.*

3. **Brevity** – *don't ramble, stay on topic. It is "cause and effect"... the better you get, the fewer words you will use, and as a result the more compelling you will be.*

4. **Style** – *develop your own style. Watch others, pick up ideas, and make adjustments... but **always be you!***

One way to learn to be a great Communicator is to watch great performers. People like Jerry Seinfeld, Celine Dion, Russell Peters, Usher... **they have mastered the above four points.** Also, they do not vary their presentation style. To make more sales, to make more money... you have to work hard at your craft... very hard. To stand out, be compelling, be consistent. The rewards are huge. Great Salespeople are paid extremely well! Why not you? **NO Excuses.**

The Communication Secret

GETTING YOUR POINT ACROSS... it is common knowledge that Communication Skills are a major part of being a great Salesperson. Let's face it, **it's all about communication.** *"Communication is not just saying what you think. It's about ensuring others hear what you mean."* We could even argue that Sales Results are more dependent upon Communication than the strength of the product itself! So let's look at the 3 main Components of Communication. The experts have established that:

1. Communication is 7%... WORDS (What you say)
2. Communication is 38%... TONE & DELIVERY (How you say it)
3. Communication is 55%... BODY LANGUAGE (How you look)

The above confirms that great Communication is not so much "what you say" (that's only 7%)... but much more "how you say it" (that's 38% + 55% = 93%!).

Here is your **ACTION STEP...** so how do you make sure that you are covering all three Components of Communication properly? There are some basics that must be adhered to every time:

1. ***Words...*** *be sure you know what you're going to say BEFORE you say it. Scripts and Dialogues need to be practiced. The alternative is "ramble-itis". This turns the Customer off.*

2. ***Tone and Delivery…*** *this is where practice pays off. Your ability to "punctuate" your words with energy and enthusiasm is critical in the Sales game. Too much or too little is disastrous. "Pick your spots" and for effect, introduce phrases and words that create emphasis.*

3. ***Body Language…*** *use "visual emotion" to make your point. Because Communication is 55% visual it is critical that the customer SEES that you are very convinced. Display your feelings. When you believe it, they will believe it.*

There is a very important footnote to this Sales Tip. Telephone Communication does not benefit from the power of point #3… Body Language. We automatically lose 55% of the formula when we are not in front of the Customer! So what's the solution? Every great telephone communicator stands up when they are on the phone. **Do not use your chair when you are on the phone.** It's as simple as that. This allows you to be more compelling. Your voice inflections and your tonality are significantly more effective when you're standing up. Don't cheat yourself on this point. **NO Excuses.**

Discovering Your Special Secret

JUST FIND IT... there is a great story about the UPS Courier Company and a discovery that changed their results. It was a small discovery, but it made a huge difference! One of their drivers pointed out that it was a lot faster when on route to turn right than to turn left. Turning right is much simpler and you don't have to deal with oncoming traffic. That one simple change meant more deliveries in less time. The suggestion... set up the delivery schedule so that "all you do is turn right". No more left turns. Doesn't sound like much, but apparently it made a huge difference. Now that's one of their rules of operation. Brilliant! What is your special secret? **What could you do that would dramatically change your results?** What new rule could you introduce to the way you do business every day?

Here is your **ACTION STEP...** Great Salespeople have their own personal set of rules. Here are some proven Sales Rules that deserve serious consideration, maybe your "right turn" is below:

Rule #1. I always find out what they need before I offer my solution. *Jumping to conclusions prematurely is a mistake. Ask extra questions just to be sure.*

Rule #2. I always close one more time than is comfortable for me... *it is amazing what that does for my customers and my results. We know that "everyone needs a nudge"... some Customers need an extra nudge.*

Rule #3. I always ask for referrals. *People love to help. When you are a satisfied Customer you feel good and you tell people about it. It's natural. Why not ask your Customers to do exactly the same thing?*

Rule #4. I always deliver more than they expect. *I am careful not to overdo it but "going that extra mile" not only makes your Customer feel better... it will make you feel better. Then it's easy to follow with Rule #3.*

One of the rules for success is to have rules for yourself. A rule is something you do every time, it is not optional. So, before you say to yourself *"I already do these four things"*, ask yourself this question, *"Are they really my rules or they just my guidelines"?* There is a huge difference! Do you follow your particular rules religiously, meaning every time, or just when it's easy? If not, start today. Once you take out the options it becomes a lot easier because you don't have to think about it... you just do it. Identify your special rule and implement it today. Pick one and never look back. **NO Excuses.**

More Important?

LOOKS WHO'S TALKING... Great Salespeople have taught themselves to avoid interruptions at all costs. We know that interruptions throw us off schedule, impact our rhythm, and generally disrupt our production. Consequently, we know that **interruptions are not a good thing.** Why is it then that we forget all this... when someone else is doing the talking!!? Why do we interrupt our customers? We make the mistake of thinking that whatever we are about to say is more important.

Here is your **ACTION STEP...** interrupting others while they are speaking is rude! Sometimes we get excited we forget that **Listening** is one of the most important Selling Skills. Here are some guidelines:

1. *The way to create great communication is to ask great questions. Keep doing that.*

2. *When your customer starts to answer... nod your head, smile, and shut up*

3. *When they are finished simply add a comment, answer their question and then... ask them another question*

4. *Everyone loves the sound of their own voice. Don't interrupt unless it's MORE IMPORTANT. Usually it isn't!*

Bonus Tip... on that rare occasion when you're unfortunate enough to be confronted by a "talker" you may need to interrupt them (sometimes you have to, or otherwise you'll have to pack a lunch!). Use this technique. Simply say, *"Interesting... and let me ask you a question"*. At that point go right back to your script. After all, the purpose of the script is to help you keep things on track. **NO Excuses.**

THE G8

THE ICEBERG APPROACH... the G8 Meeting was held in my little town of Huntsville, Ontario in June, 2010. Eight leaders of the economic world all came together in a town of 15,000 people. U.S. President Obama and Canada's Prime Minister Harper were among them. So our beautiful little resort town became a very different place for a short time. The amazing thing is that even with the addition of thousands of armed forces personnel & police officers & helicopters, etc., etc., etc... **everything ran very, very smoothly!** They were prepared for any Crisis...and there were no visible problems. SMOOTH AS SILK.

Here is your **ACTION STEP...** when you are in **"Crisis Mode"**, how smoothly does your business run? Our customers and our business associates expect us to take the ICEBERG APPROACH:

1. *10% of your activity should show above the surface*

2. *90% of your activity is underwater, behind the scenes*

3. ***Nobody cares** how busy you are/how are stressed you are*

4. *If you show stress, it steals from your professionalism*

5. The KEY is to... be calm and make a point of keeping the "behind the scenes" activities to yourself

6. The results are all that matters. Keep the rest "underwater"

BONUS TIP: just watch those around you when they are floundering. Watch how foolish and unprofessional that looks. No drama & less stress = more money! **NO Excuses.**

<u>**What do they see?**</u>

THE 15 SECOND CHECKUP... many Salespeople spend hours preparing their presentations, practicing their delivery, and having flashy graphics and handouts to impress their Customers. Having done all that, they forget the most important part of their package... **the initial impression they create** when their Customers first evaluate them. How strong is the first impression you provide? Presumably everyone starts on a "level playing field". It either goes up or down from there.

Here is your **ACTION STEP...** recognize the following truism... *"Know that you are being judged at all times... Know that the first judgment is often the most lasting".* It only takes about 15 seconds for your Customer to form an opinion about you. This is called the **"15 Second Checkup".** Here are the basic criteria you must pass:

1. *Dress well (under-dressing or sloppiness is inexcusable)*

2. *Always be smiling (what's the alternative?)*

3. *Have a solid handshake (have your friends critique you)*

4. *Present a strong physiology (exude energy, be confident, good eye contact)*

5. *Pay attention to your personal grooming (be attractive!)*

6. *Practice an "economy of words" (say less, it's more powerful)*

Did you pass the test? All great Salespeople work on the first impression they create on an ongoing basis. It never stops. Trying to change a bad first impression is really hard work, so do it right the first time. Make it easy on yourself... do the **"15 Second Checkup" on yourself** every day. You are on stage and it's Showtime! **NO Excuses.**

Chapter 4
The Power of Questions

Wisdom from Earl & Henry

MIND POWER... when Earl Nightingale introduced his wildly successful book, ***The Strangest Secret***, over 50 years ago a lot of people paid attention. His "secret" was very simple - ***"You become what you think about most of the time".*** Of course, this created a tremendous amount of debate because there are always naysayers when an idea that profound is introduced. Nowadays this is a very readily accepted premise. From there it's not much of a transition to buy into the theory that... **in Sales, success is 90% Mindset (IE: what you are thinking about).**

Earl Nightingale never said that he invented this idea. Henry Ford said the same thing a different way earlier in the century. Mr. Ford said that *"If you think you can or if you think you can't... either way you are right".* He went on to say *"It is the thinking that makes it so".*

Let's put two of these theories together. If you *"become what you think about most of the time"* and if *"sales success is 90% mindset"*... then **it is critical for you to have control of your thoughts every day.**

Here is your **ACTION STEP...** ask yourself these great questions on ongoing basis:

1. *What do I think about most of the day?*

2. *What do I say when I talk to myself... does it add to or subtract from how I want to feel?*

3. *What impact does my environment have on me?*

4. *What do I do daily to refill my "mental toughness tank"?*

5. *Do I accept responsibility or do I take on the "victim" role?*

Sometimes you are so busy keeping things under control that you forget to do the most important thing of all... that is, **look after yourself.** You need to *"Be a vicious guard dog at the door of your mind".* Equally important is for you to be thinking the right things all the time. Selling requires energy, skill, commitment, and most of all **powerful thinking to create a powerful mindset. NO Excuses.**

Push or Pull?

SWIMMING UPSTREAM?... There is an old joke that goes like this: *A guy tells his psychiatrist, "I always have this weird dream at night. I am locked in a room with a door on which there is a sign. I try to push it with all my strength, but no matter how hard I try, it won't budge. The psychiatrist muses, "Interesting." But tell me what does the sign on the door say? The guy replies, "It says PULL"!!!* Rather humorous, and at the same time there is a great message here for Salespeople. Is it possible that you are "pushing" when it would be much more productive to "pull"?

Here is your **ACTION STEP...** there's always room for improvement. Even the best Salesperson needs to step back and take look at their approach periodically. Here are some **examples of pushing instead of pulling. Step back and ask yourself, are you:**

1. *Fighting the fact that Social Media is here to stay? The world is changing.*

2. *Conversely, spending too much time in front of the computer "getting ready to get going" and not doing your real job?*

3. *Expecting your Past Clients and Center of Influence to send you business without personally asking them to do so?*

4. *Working too long with "on the fence" prospects who never make a decision?*

5. *Thinking that you are talking to enough people every day about business even though your results never get better? Selling is still a "people business". Don't expect advertising, mail outs, and e-mails to replace personal contact.*

Sometimes we confuse persistence with common sense. Check the sign on the door... are you pushing vs. pulling? Consider some of the above options. Do you need to revisit your current strategy? Take this 2 part acid test... *Q. #1 Am I "swimming upstream"? Am I ignoring the obvious? & Q. #2 Have I forgotten my big picture goal? Wasn't it to help people who need me so I can earn a living and reach my goals?*

Have an honest look at some of the things you are doing on a day-to-day basis. Changing your strategy doesn't mean you were wrong... it just might be that it is time to adjust your approach. **NO Excuses.**

Start by Asking

START BY ASKING... most Salespeople know two things for sure...

#1. I need to Ask for Referrals more often AND

#2. Sometimes I just don't feel comfortable Asking for Referrals.

Here is your **ACTION STEP...** Let's look at some simple answers to the question, "When should I ask for referrals and what's the easiest way to do that?":

1. *Ask for Referrals after you have provided value... not before. When you give value to your Customers, they are much more inclined to reciprocate... and they will give back.*

2. *Ask for Referrals when you know they are pleased with the service you have provided. A simple approach is the direct approach... "Mr. Customer, how do you feel about this sale/your purchase/the service we have provided?"*

3. *The best time to Ask for Referrals is right after the sale is made. When the chemistry is right, take advantage of it. Simply put, why shouldn't you? People love to help*

4. *Get comfortable asking the same way every time. Take five minutes and write down the question you want to ask. Here's an example... "As you know, I am always looking for more people to help*

in my business... who do you know who needs my help to (your product/service) right now?".

The Salespeople who do not Ask for Referrals consistently follow a dangerous assumption. They believe that when the opportunity arises their Customers will automatically send business their way. Big mistake! This is the story they tell themselves because they believe that Asking for Referrals is "being pushy".... *"My Customers have a lot going on in their lives, and sending me referrals is not the first thing on their list."* It's your job to remind them that you are very effective at providing value. You just did it for them! Ask and you shall receive. **NO Excuses.**

90 Days Gone

GPS TIME... Every 90 days, all businesses need to turn on their **"Results GPS"** to see where they are. No matter what you are selling, it is critical to step back and take a look to see how you are doing. WHY?... because *"how do you know if you're going to get there if you don't look at the road map periodically"?*

Those who do not do a <u>routine</u> Quarterly Review are in denial... so let's hold our production up to the mirror and face reality.

Here is your **ACTION STEP....** There are Four parts to a quarterly review, so ask yourself:

1. *Where should I be right now? (refer to your annual plan)*
2. *What have I sold so far? (the #s don't lie)*
3. *What adjustments do I need to make immediately?*
4. *What 2-3 clear Action Steps can I create to make the changes?*

Bonus Tip #1: if you don't have an annual plan... immediately create one.

Bonus Tip #2: get someone to hold you accountable to your Action Steps. Trying to do it on your own is stopping you from growing. Get your ego of the way. Did you know E.G.O. also stands for *"eliminates growth opportunities"?* **NO Excuses.**

Name That Tune

JINGLE BELLS.... Finish this sentence. "Jingle Bells, Jingle Bells, Jingle ....". I already know you have answered "... all the way". Do you know why you were able to do that? Because, you've done it so many times that it has become internalized, and you will never forget it. Repetition is the Salesperson's best friend!

Here is you **ACTION STEP...** *make a list of the various phrases and questions that you should be using but sometimes forget.* Read them out loud, over and over and over again. Practice using phrases like...

1. *"No problem, could you tell me more about that?" (fact finding)*

2. *"Are you already to go ahead now?" (closing)*

3. *"Let's do the right thing and..." (leading)*

4. *"Why would you want to do that?" (objection handling)*

5. *"May I explain?" (taking control)*

Create your own "Jingle Bells"...and have them ready so they come out automatically. Repetition will make you rich! **NO Excuses.**

Verbosity

BLAH, BLAH, BLAH.... Many years ago there was a hit song by Ernie K. Doe called *"You Talk Too Much"*. In 2010, singer Ke$ha came out with one entitled *"Blah, Blah, Blah"*. Same message, different tune. Most salespeople are guilty of Telling and not Selling! The problem is that when we get nervous, we just keep talking... not a good idea. There is a solution.

Here is your **ACTION STEP.....**

1. *Remember that the best Salespeople ask lots of QUESTIONS*

2. *To create conversation, ask lots of Open Ended questions*

3. *Open ended questions often start with:* ***Who, What, Where, When, Why, & How***

4. *As a reminder, put these 6 magic words on a sheet of paper (in big letters) and stick it on the wall*

5. *Start asking and stop telling*

This could be the Most Important Sales Strategy you will ever get from me. It will make you rich! Read it again, okay? (Surprise! There was yet another question). **NO Excuses.**

How to Say it Better

REPHRASE YOUR QUESTION... there are hundreds of great selling techniques. One of the ones that is very, very high on the list is the **"power of questions".** When mastering the finer points of selling, it is important to "master asking great questions". This Sales Tip is all about taking a common sales question and making sure you are using the right words.

Here is your **ACTION STEP...** Become powerful at rephrasing.

Frequently Salespeople want to know how their Prospects are going to evaluate the various Salespeople that they interview. It is a good strategy. Find out what they're looking for and then provide just that.

> The most common way this question is asked is:
>
> *"What are you looking for in a Salesperson?"* The problem with this question is that we usually get the stock answers that really don't tell us much: *honest, hard-working, knowledgeable, etc...* very nebulous and not measurable.
>
> Here is a better way to ask the same question:
>
> *"How are you going to decide which Salesperson you choose?"* This forces the client to actually put some thought into their answer. Whatever they reply will be much more meaningful than the answers above.

Bonus Tip: if there are benefits you bring to the table that they haven't mentioned in their reply, you can introduce those by asking the following... *"How important is it to you that I also...*(then tell them what else you do that is valuable to them)?"

Learn how to rephrase some of your questions so that they generate more useful answers. Not only will you be helping your customer make the right decision, you will also be improving your results! **NO Excuses.**

Social Media Marketing

WATCH OUT FOR THE TRAP... There is no doubt that Social Media has replaced a lot of the marketing that in the past was done using traditional print media. In most cases it is much more economical... the question still remains as to how effective it is. Some Salespeople become very defensive when this point is brought up and respond with things like... *"I got a deal just the other day from the Internet... don't tell me it doesn't work!"* There is a great book on the market that really helps deal with the issue of how to skilfully employ the Internet. Check it out... ***Trust Agents: Using the Web to Build Influence, Improve Reputation, and Earn Trust,*** by Chris Brogan and Julien Smith. It is really good. At one point near the end of the book they caution the reader to not get too wrapped up in "chasing rainbows". They use a great metaphor to ask... *"Does it matter how many people are walking around your store if they are not buying anything?"* Brogan and Smith warn us not to get seduced by the "someday they might buy" myth.

Here is your **ACTION STEP...** great Salespeople never lose sight of the primary goal of RESULTS & REVENUE. Here are some great questions to ask yourself every day...

1. *Who can I talk to today to help me make money this week?*

2. *Considering my goals, is what I'm doing right now the very best use of my time?*

3. *Am I focusing on finding and working with 30 day customers, or just anyone who comes along?*

4. *When was the last time I reviewed my Personal Goals? And, what are my REAL priorities?*

Effective time management is all about working towards your top priorities. This Tip is really focusing on two main messages... #1. Use Social Media to your advantage but don't let it consume you AND #2. While it is important to develop customers for the future, don't forget to select a few who are doing business right now! Remember... RESULTS & REVENUE. **NO Excuses.**

The Hockey Coach

RESISTING THE UNCOMFORTABLE... one of my long-time clients has a very accomplished teenage son who is a terrific goalie in minor hockey. Recently they hired a very well-known Goalie Coach to help him improve his skills. The exercise was a great success. The Coach asked the son to make some changes. To his credit, he did... and they worked! There was some resistance along the way. When someone is getting you to change the way you do things, and do things differently, **there is bound to be some resistance.** When we resist change it doesn't mean we are not "coachable"... it just means that we are more comfortable doing things the old way. **We resist the uncomfortable.** How much resistance do you have to changing the way you do business? To the way you Sell?

Here is your **ACTION STEP...** one of the best parts about my job is watching people grow. Sometimes while conducting Seminars and Personal Coaching I run into some fairly standard resistances. Ask yourself, are you resisting any of the following:

1. *Prospecting for new business every day? Prospecting in the morning?*

2. *Revising/shortening your listing presentation?*

3. *Using scripts? Practicing scripts?*

4. *Writing out & learning Objection Handlers... no more "winging it"?*

5. *Reviewing/writing out your Personal Goals daily?*

6. *Hiring a great Coach who will help you get there?*

Resistance to change is understandable... **resistance to change that can improve your life is not understandable.** Doing all of the above items will change your life. Think about it and stop resisting. Take on something today that will change your results. Do what you know you need to do. **NO Excuses.**

Simplicity is Best

WINNING ISN'T COMPLICATED... somewhere in the mid-90s there was a great basketball movie produced, starring Nick Nolte, called "Blue Chips". A sign on the wall in the home team's dressing room read "Don't Complicate Winning". In other words, Keep It Simple. I am fortunate to have a long time client named Bryan Black, in Aurora, Ontario. Bryan has a tremendous Corporate Business background. He has always treated his Sales Career as a business.... and a simple business at that. Recently we were discussing his philosophy on how he keeps his business simple.

Here is your **ACTION STEP...** *Do as Bryan says.* "There is a simple cycle. I break it down into four steps":

1. *Where am I right now? (my current business results)*
2. *Where do I want to go? (my new targets/goals)*
3. *What do I have to do to get there?*
4. *What are the steps required to make this happen?*

Bryan does very well in business. He focuses on what he wants to accomplish, goes out and does it, and then sets new targets. This is a cycle that he repeats over and over. Do not complicate winning... keep it simple. Use the above formula and don't get sidetracked with minutia. **NO Excuses.**

Chapter 5
Developing Sales Systems

Who's in Charge?

HELP ME!!!... Every great Salesperson has moments of panic and fear. One that comes up frequently when writing a new Business Plan is *"Never mind increasing my results... I don't even know how I'm going to be able to repeat what I did last year!!!"* Don't allow yourself to be overwhelmed, it is all about how you approach each day.

Here is your **ACTION STEP...** three things to do:

1. *Remember that "No One is coming to the Rescue!"... YOU, and you alone, are in charge of your results. Take responsibility and stay away from all the drama.*

2. *Take your annual targets for your various production items and break them down into monthly totals.*

3. *Now here's the real key to your success... break the monthly targets down to weekly totals. Just focus on what you need to accomplish this week. (read "The Power of Focus" by Canfield, Hansen, & Hewitt for more insight)*

The key is to not look at the Big target... take baby steps every day and the year will take care of itself. Certainly you've heard the quip "How do you eat an elephant?" The answer is simple, "One bite at a time!" **NO Excuses.**

Fussing for Nothing

GUILT FREE... in his famous best seller ***First Things First***, author Stephen Covey talks about always dealing with what's important. The title is rather self-explanatory. The strength of the book, however, is in the ways Covey helps us work on putting our REAL priorities front and center. Now for a slightly different twist... this Sales Tip is for all those great Salespeople who are guilty of... *"beating themselves up far more than is necessary!"* I suspect that covers almost everyone.

Here is your **ACTION STEP...** Mr. Covey says when looking at your goals and your achievements... *"do not fuss with where you wanted to be, rather look at where you are... compared to where you were!"* [Hmmmm... read that line again]

In other words, look at the **exciting GAP** you have created between 'Then' & 'Now'. Here's an example:

1. *How many sales did I have this time last year?*

2. *How many sales have I had so far this year?*

3. *Calculate the difference... chances are you are ahead. This Is **Your Success Gap.** Congratulations!*

4. *Critical Point: even if you're not where you wanted to be, you are still way ahead of where you were.*

Pat yourself on the back, take credit for your progress, and adjust your strategy to move even further ahead.

Here's a great new affirmation for you: *"Beating myself up has disappeared from my life. I grow every day."* **NO Excuses.**

Action and Attraction

THE SECRET... a few years ago the Law of Attraction was re-popularized in Rhonda Byrne's book/video, ***The Secret***. It became an amazing success. It awakened millions of people to the possibility that great opportunities and rewards could be theirs by having a plan and an open mind to attracting success. The naysayers, of course, jumped all over this saying that nothing would happen by itself. The fact is that "The Secret" never said that it would... the message was all about being positive, having a plan, having the right mindset, and... **TAKING ACTION!**

Here is your **ACTION STEP...**

DO... DON'T JUST DREAM!

Famous Ohio State NCAA Coach Woody Hayes had a great line. Woody said, *"Hope is not a Strategy".* Anyone naïve enough to think that the Law of Attraction is all about buying a lottery ticket and sitting in your lazy-boy chair waiting for your winnings to arrive is "a bit short upstairs".

Here is one of my all-time favorite mantras...*"The secret to success in selling is creating an equality between your activities and your goals."*

If your goal is to sell 100 units of a product over a period of one year then you must be prepared to create enough activities to make that happen. It is a simple application of the Law of Cause and Effect..... "do and you get!".

So here's two huge questions for you, ***"Am I conducting enough Activities on a day-to-day basis to reach the Results in my business plan [i.e.: my goals]? Do the 2 add up?"*** If YES, then keep going... if NO, pick up the pace! **NO Excuses.**

Aren't They Amazing?

While watching the **Winter or Summer Olympics...** it's hard not to be inspired by the "price" the athletes have paid to get to that level of excellence. They have given "their all" just to qualify to compete!

I'm reminded of the Salespeople that look at a peer who is overachieving and say, *"Well, if that's what you have to do to succeed... it's certainly not worth it to me! I'm happy where I am".* They just came from a course where they teach: Excuses 101.

Here is your **ACTION STEP...**

1. *Decide what you want*
2. *Find someone who's already done it*
3. *Do exactly what they do (model them)*
4. *Ignore the people who "chirp" at you on the way by!*

Be an Olympic Champion in your chosen field!!! Start by telling yourself that "not doing it is not an option". **NO Excuses.**

Another Secret to Winning

THE SPEED BUMP... while driving through a peaceful neighbourhood recently I was confronted with a series of unavoidable speed bumps. As I was in a hurry, I found them rather irritating. At that point I had to reflect on why they were there... they had a purpose. **Speed Bumps are designed to slow us down when we are not paying attention!** Sometimes we're so busy "going fast" we miss the point.

Here is your **ACTION STEP...** aren't there times when we should introduce some "mental speed bumps" in our day to day approach to Selling? Here are some examples of when we should introduce "mental speed bumps" to help us be more effective before we get in front of the Client. Take the extra time to:

1. *Prepare thoroughly for an important client presentation. Don't just rush out the door all out of breath!*

2. *Rehearse a particular objection handler you are anticipating receiving.*

3. *When you're not sure about something...ask for advice. EGO, be gone!*

4. *Get everything ready for tomorrow... your prospecting, your 'to-do' list, even your wardrobe. "My day begins the night before."*

5. *Track your numbers once a week. Stop guessing where you are.*

Bonus Tip: Make sure you also take the time to add this last very important "speed bump"... ***appreciate how good you really are getting at the Selling Game.*** Pat yourself on the back. Acknowledge that you definitely are growing! **NO Excuses.**

How to Get Out of the Rut?

STUCK IN A RUT?... Even the best Salespeople run into periods where their production does not seem to be moving forward. It's frustrating and sometimes it's like running into a brick wall. The harder you try the more things do not seem to go your way. You feel "snake bit", and even your confidence level can slip. Neither of these two reactions are valid, but it still can be disconcerting no matter how long you have been in the Sales business. Let me share some answers that certainly have worked for me.

Here is your **ACTION STEP...** the first thing is that you need to do is to *"slow down in order to speed up".* This means you've got to look at what is going on with you and your business every day:

1. *Be open to new ideas on how to run your business (Is it now time to introduce one or two of those changes you have been putting off?)*

2. *Focus more on your "NOW" business. Make sure that your Hot Leads are getting your full attention. Call them more often, versus less often*

3. *Book one day off per week. It could simply be that you are burned out. Give yourself some planned breaks, because we all need something to look forward to*

4. *Ask yourself... what things have I been doing that I should be saying NO to? (Examples: do I have any Clients who are going nowhere?)*

5. *Ask yourself... have I stopped doing some of the things I normally did when things were going well? (Daily exercise, getting enough sleep, preparing properly for appointments, practicing my presentation, lead generating, etc.)*

6. *Spend 30 minutes per day "ON" your business versus "IN" your business. Step back and take a look every day. Be your own CEO once a day.*

One thing for sure, **when you are "in a rut"... more of the same *is not the answer*.** It's time to be Proactive versus Reactive. Look for solutions that will stay with you, not short-term "desperado" fixes. It's the Big Picture that you need to address. **NO Excuses.**

Check Out This Question

WHAT ARE THE CLUES?... There's an old joke that starts off with the following question... *"How many people work for you?".* The humorous answer is... *"Let me see now... oh, about half of them!".* It got me thinking about how the answer would go for *"How many Salespeople actually work?".* Hopefully the answer would not be... *"half of them".* The fact is that there are as many different Work Habits as there are Salespeople. We do know one thing... Success leaves Clues. There is a definite pattern that Successful Salespeople follow. **What are the clues?**

Here is your **ACTION STEP...** Successful Salespeople leave all the regular clues behind them. Things like... consistently prospecting in one form or another, consistently showing up on time for work, and consistently being available for their customers. No surprises here. Now, let's look at some of the more "hidden clues" that aren't quite so obvious. **Successful Salespeople...**

*Clue #1. Focus only on **NOW business.** They have a clear list of their top leads, they prequalify better, they don't waste time on "time vampires".*

*Clue #2. **Practice for 30 minutes,** 5 days a week. They make the time because they know this is the secret to developing superior skills.*

Clue #3. Have a clear ***Business Plan*** *(yearly, monthly,... even weekly!) and they track their progress regularly.*

Clue #4. Have a presentation that clearly ***demonstrates the differences*** *between them and the competition. They are Great Presenters.*

Clue #5. Are ***Coachable and Accountable.*** *They have a "NO Excuses" mentality and are 100% responsible for their growth & their results.*

Clue #6. Work on ***improving their Mindset daily.*** *They never forget that Sales Success is 90% Mindset & Attitude.*

Clue #7. Put in the ***extra effort*** *that separates them from everyone else. This includes appearance, presentation, sales skills, commitment.*

Bonus Point: all of the above clues require a different Level of Commitment. **The difference between being average and *being great* is creating an intensity in your work day that is consistent and unrelenting.** The good news is that to pay the price for great results, you don't really have to do that much more than the average Salesperson. You just have to do it at a higher level. That's why Clue #7 is so important. You don't have to work that much harder... you just have to work hard when you are actually working. **NO Excuses.**

Back Scratching

HELP THEM / HELP YOU... if you check your Past Clients and Center of Influence list often you will find quite a few people who are in business on their own... entrepreneurs, just like you. One of the best ways to develop a referrals system is to send referrals to those entrepreneurs in your database. This can be done easily, economically, and in high volume.

Here is your **ACTION STEP...** let's say for example you have someone in your database who owns a Muffler Repair Shop. Here's the idea:

1. *Approach that business owner and see what discount coupons they offer to promote volume [e.g.: $50 off on a new muffler system]*

2. *Suggest to them that you will send out coupons to everyone in your database to help promote their business [they will jump at your offer!]*

3. *Include the coupon in your next mailing or publish it in your next monthly newsletter*

4. *Next month find another similar opportunity and share it with your whole database again*

This is a WIN/WIN for everyone! The entrepreneur will love you for it and no doubt will reciprocate on an ongoing basis. Next, you are giving everyone in your database an opportunity for a discount. And lastly, you'll get more business because of it. You can't lose.

Start doing this every month. Believe me, *"What goes around comes around."* **NO Excuses.**

Sales Killer #11

RAINY DAY $$$... Sales Killer # 11 is not having any **"Rainy Day Savings".** Great Salespeople make great decisions... in both their business and personal lives. If you don't have some money put aside it can affect the quality of your decisions. Here are two "acid-test" questions: #1. How attached do you become to a weak lead if you are attached to the outcome? AND #2. How objective can you be if you are desperate for a deal? Get yourself out of that stressful scenario.

Here is your **ACTION STEP...** in the next 60-90 days you are going to get some pretty exciting commission cheques. Commit to the following:

1. *Decide on a specific amount of money to take off each cheque*

2. *Set up a place to "stash" that cash $$$$*

3. *No matter what, keep your word and set that money aside*

4. *Build up your personal "Rainy Day Savings", you deserve the FREEDOM it will give you*

Even if you only save $100/deal you and your customers will be much better off. Next time you have a stressful situation, you will make better decisions and your customers will receive better advice. **NO Excuses.**

Pull A Card Out Now!

BUSINESS CARD WISDOM... everybody has a business card. We see lots of them as we go through our day-to-day activities. The main reason a business card exists is so people can be reminded of us and **know how to contact us.** There are some very basic common sense items we must keep in mind when we are creating our business card design. Trying to make it more than that will make it difficult for our potential clients to reach us.

Here is your **ACTION STEP...** *look at your business card right now.* If one of the main purposes of a business card is for people to be able to contact you, ask yourself this question... **"can people get in touch with me easily?"** Be sure that the answer is YES:

1. *Is your e-mail address highly legible and easy to find? (Some business cards do not even have one!)*

2. *Does the main phone # stand out?*

3. *Is your card "clutter free"? Keep it simple, and eliminate unnecessary information & artwork*

4. *Using a slogan? You decide... just remember that no one is going to choose you just because of a catchy phrase*

5. *Using a photograph? Your choice... just make sure it didn't come out of your high school yearbook!*

Bonus Idea: ask one of your friends to look at your current business card and see if it passes the above criteria. They may see or not see something you don't. The main question is, can clients contact you easily using the media of their choice (i.e.: e-mail, telephone, website)? Don't be a Secret Agent. **NO Excuses.**

Chapter 6
Being Prepared!

Mirror This

Mirror, Mirror on the Wall... certain things we should not forget. Sometimes the most important tasks, values, and ideas get lost in the heat of the moment. Sometimes we think about them after the fact and "wish we weren't so forgetful". Reality is, you're not forgetful... there's just a lot of "stuff" going on. There are certain key items in your life that deserve your best attention.

Here's your **ACTION STEP...** one of the things you look at for a few minutes every day is your bathroom mirror... here's a great Sales Tip:

1. *Put a short note on your bathroom mirror... including things like:*

    - ***your personal goals***
    - ***your business targets for this month***
    - ***your favourite affirmations***
    - ***your favourite "ask everyone for business" line***
    - ***your next "date" with someone special***

2. *Repeat them out loud every AM & PM. Internalize them!*

Make these "most important tasks, values, and ideas of who you are" the areas of your highest focus. Never lose sight of why you are doing what you do.

Add this affirmation to your list... *"I am very focused on what's important to me... everyday!!!"* **NO Excuses.**

Your Success Cycle

YOUR SUCCESS CYCLE… is there a pattern to your results, or do they come as a surprise? Do you have a system for running your Sales Business? Here's the Big Question… are your results predictable? They definitely should be!

Here is your **ACTION STEP…** Success doesn't happen by itself. There is an actual Success Cycle that you can create, when you:

1. *Set your* ***Business Goals***
2. *Isolate the* ***Activities*** *needed to get the job done*
3. *Create a* ***Daily Schedule*** *to support these Activities*
4. ***Implement*** *your routine on a daily basis ("git 'er done")*
5. *Work on your* ***Sales Skills*** *30 minutes every single day*
6. *Measure your* ***Results*** *and adjust your Activities*

And, no surprise … This approach has a 100% Success rate!!! The stronger and more consistent your Success Cycle, the more you will sell. Get started. **NO Excuses.**

What're You Waiting For?

ARE YOU READY YET?... I came across a great thought recently from songwriter James Gordon:

"It is not that some people have willpower and some do not. It is that some people are ready to change and others are not".

We all say we want to change certain things, but most Salespeople are not ready to change anything... at least "not just yet". Sound familiar?

Here is your **ACTION STEP...** when you did your own personal Annual Sales Plan (you do have one, right?) I suspect you changed your Results targets from last year, didn't you? If you did, then you needed to change your Daily Activities to support those new Results targets, right?

1. *No matter where you are in your business year, take a look at the way you are doing things now compared to the approach you used 12 months ago.*

2. *What have you changed? Make one permanent change to your routine today... no more "getting ready". Pick out that one item and write it down. Put it in your schedule.*

TODAY is THE DAY. **NO Excuses.**

Shiny Enough?

THE SHINY SHOES... here's a great question for you. If you were to compare your business operation to a pair of shoes, how shiny would they be? One of the many bright lights in my Coaching roster recently compared her business to a pair of shiny shoes. She said *"I want them to look like patent leather... not something that I have to 'spit and shine' every morning".* So what does your business look like?... Patent leather or spit and shine?

Here is your **ACTION STEP...** *"spit and shine"* means that you are always cleaning up your operation instead of always being in "ready mode". Adopt the right approach... the *"patent leather"* approach, where:

1. *You exercise five times a week, so your energy level is at its highest and best*

2. *You fill your mind with positive influences every day (CDs, books, etc.)*

3. *You practice your scripts and dialogs daily so your customers see you at your finest*

4. *Your materials, your attitude, and your appearance are always top-notch*

5. *You always "get ready" the night before so you are off and running on time every day*

6. *You have a Sense of Urgency in everything you do. People are attracted to your energy!*

These are the things a Superstar does every day. Have a look at your "shoes". You may not need to replace them, but if you look at the above list you may need to give them a good "polish". Do what you need to do to stand out... the rewards will be huge! **NO Excuses.**

How did he do That?

NEVER TOO LATE... the Toronto Blue Jays acquired utility baseball player José Bautista late in 2009. At the time he was 28 years old, had been in the league five years, and was considered a "throw in" to complete a larger trade. Quite understandable, considering he was drafted in the 20th round by the Pittsburgh Pirates and subsequently played for four other teams before coming to Toronto. No one thought much about it because at that point his career statistics were anything but remarkable. **Then something happened!** Mr. Bautista became a star almost overnight in 2010. He had 54 home runs that year. He currently leads the major leagues with 31 home runs halfway through the 2011 season. His batting average is in excess of .330. He received more votes for the 2011 All-Star game than any other player in history! On top of all that, he has taken on a new role with his team and has become the team leader. So what happened?... Simply put, he says, *"I started working on my game with much more intention. I decided if I was going to be an overachiever I would have to make some changes. Plus... I got a lot of help making those changes".*

Here is your **ACTION STEP...** the message here is that "even after several years in the league" any Salesperson can generate significantly improved results! You are never stuck at one level! Needless to say, **there is a price to pay.** What is that price?...

1. *Make the decision that you're NOT going to settle for your current production*

2. *Decide that you're going to PAY THE PRICE, no matter what!*

3. *CRITICAL: Work on your Sales Skills for a minimum of 30 minutes every morning before the day begins. NO Excuses (AND there is no short cut on this)*

4. *Work all the time that you work and take scheduled time off so you don't get burned out*

5. *Hire a Coach... as the expression goes, "If you see a turtle on a fence post, you can be sure he had help getting there".*

It's Never Too Late! José Bautista's story is very inspirational and considering the skill required, his turnaround is quite remarkable. Regardless, all Salespeople can write the same story for themselves. **Decide, plan, act, and pay the price.** As a final note, this does not mean you have to give up your personal life. It means you have to give up your current life... because it's not getting you to that next level. Even if you have been in the Sales Game for a long time, it doesn't mean you can't change your results dramatically! Follow these steps. **NO Excuses.**

Advice That is Easy to Accept

HALL OF FAME WISDOM... former second baseman Roberto Alomar was voted into the Baseball Hall of Fame in Cooperstown, NY. The baseball HOF is generally considered the toughest one to enter. Of the millions of kids who play baseball, of the thousands who do it professionally, of the hundreds who do it in the major leagues, only a very select few make it to the Hall of Fame. When asked the inevitable "secret to your success?" question, Alomar responded very specifically and without hesitation. He said that it was one thing. He said *"The best thing that ever happened to me was to play for manager Cito Gaston. What Cito did was to let me be myself".* That was his "magic pill". It doesn't mean he didn't take direction... it does mean he was allowed to... **"Be Myself".**

Here is your **ACTION STEP...** I Have a Speaking Coach. The best advice I got from my Coach was the following... *"Study other Speakers, learn what they do well, and then see if you should adapt those things into who you already are.* ***Most of all don't try to be someone else... Be Yourself".*** Great Salespeople focus on who they are and present that image to their Customers. Some thoughts and questions as you consider this concept:

1. *Do you have the courage and the self-confidence to "Be Yourself"?*

2. *Who are you? Write out a list of your strengths on a piece of paper. You already have numerous skills,*

write them down so you can articulate and focus on them.

3. *Decide what is the best way* ***for you*** *to display those strengths and skills.*

4. *Do you work on your skills every day? Hall of Famers don't go to work every day until they have practiced first.*

5. *Don't let periodic "errors on the playing field" deter you from "being yourself". Mistakes happen, that doesn't mean you should change who you are.*

Be proud of who you are, what you have accomplished, and where you are headed. Too many Salespeople go through life questioning their every step. Have the courage of your convictions and don't try to be anybody other than yourself. You're just fine the way you are. Keep growing. **NO Excuses.**

Call 911

ACCEPTING HELP... there is no Salesperson who does not need help at different stages in their career. We need help in improving our sales skills, we need help in improving our time management, we help in dealing with rejection, etc. etc. etc. As a wise man said to me one day... *"Being comfortable asking for help is important, but it's more important to be comfortable accepting help when it is offered".* That's not always easy to do. Sometimes when we are having trouble "keeping our heads above water" we foolishly resist the "life preserver" that is thrown our way.

Here is your **ACTION STEP...** some people are significantly more Coachable than others. My observation is that the higher your level of self-confidence, the more Coachable you are. Individuals who have low self-confidence are generally very resistant to outside advice. Defense mechanisms kick in. Here are some ideas on ACCEPTING HELP:

1. *Ignore the source... just because the source isn't at the highest level of expertise, doesn't mean the advice isn't worthwhile. Be open-minded.*

2. *Work hard at keeping your EGO out of the way. The "don't you know who I am?" mentality doesn't work very well here.*

3. *Consider what is being offered and take this approach... rather than deciding why "that won't work"... look for ways to "make it work".*

4. *If the advice offered still makes you sceptical, ask questions to get some clarity… "How did you come up with that idea?", "Have you seen this approach work elsewhere?", "How would you suggest I implement this?". There might be a diamond in there!*

We have all seen situations where seemingly outlandish ideas and advice became highly successful endeavors (eg: Google and Facebook). If the advice that was offered along the way had been totally ignored and/or the recipients were not Coachable, either they would never have become reality or… someone else would have implemented the concepts themselves. **The most successful Salespeople are always looking for advice and new ideas.** Be open to help wherever you go. There are some great ideas out there on how to close your next Sale. *"Ask and you shall receive".* **NO Excuses.**

The Breaking Point

THAT'S IT!... I'M CHANGING... I came across a great quote the other day from author and radio personality Dave Ramsey. He was talking about that "breaking point", when we get fed up enough and make a change. Dave said

"Not until the pain of staying the same is greater than the pain of change will you embrace change".

This is a very powerful realization, and like much wisdom is surprisingly fundamental. We put up with things in our lives for as long as we can stand it and then when we reach the **"breaking point"** we make a change. Example: If your car keeps breaking down and costs too much to fix, eventually you decide to buy a new car.

Here is your **ACTION STEP...** change is never easy but it becomes much easier when we have "had enough"! Some examples are: our clothes don't fit so we decide to lose weight, a relationship becomes unhappy so we terminate it, our income is insufficient so we work harder.

The question then becomes, ***How can you accelerate the process of change so your breaking point arrives earlier?*** Interesting concept isn't it? This would improve your life faster. Discover ways to speed things up:

1. *Review your minimum standards... are you tolerating situations, conditions or individuals who do not "make the cut"? Should you "raise the bar"?*

2. *Consider the Big Picture. Is the way things are going today going to get you where you want to go?*
3. *Review your level of self confidence about making changes. If it is not strong enough, align yourself with a Mentor who can help you **"build up your courage enough to escape your current universe".***

4. *Critical Point: Put a plan together with specific Action Steps that will move you forward. Perform these on a daily basis to help you introduce these all-important changes (baby steps work really well here). "Progress, not perfection".*

5. *Screw up your courage and get on with it! That's the difference between "breaking out" and just thinking about it.*

Consider this metaphor... *five birds are sitting on a telephone wire. Two birds decide to fly south. How many are left? Most people would say three. Actually, all five are left.* You see, deciding to fly isn't the same as doing it. Don't just "decide to fly"... jump off the wire and start flapping your wings. Staying on the wire is not acceptable. **NO Excuses.**

Day Surgery

HIGH STANDARDS... recently I had occasion to lose a day's production because of some needed "Day Surgery". No big deal, all was well, and it did give me an opportunity to see how the outside world operates. Sometimes we get so wrapped up in being Salespeople we forget there is a whole different world out there. The medical profession is an example. Needless to say, they have amazing **"minimum standards".** They have to... otherwise we would die!

Here is your **ACTION STEP...** as I lay on the operating table I asked myself, *"How would I react in Day Surgery if the nurses and doctors didn't have incredibly high minimum standards? What if they looked unkempt, or were rude, or seemed angry, incompetent, etc. etc.".* Scary! We would be indignant... and very vocal in our displeasure. Your own personal minimum standards are what "sets the bar" for your Sales results. If you have low standards... no one buys from you!

Here are some **minimum standards** questions for you:

1. *Do I always look the part?*
2. *Do I put my personal feelings aside?*
3. *Am I always on time?*
4. *Do I use scripts or do I just "ramble on"?*

5. *Do I work on my Sales Skills or do I just take mandatory training because I have to?*
6. *Do I have an Accountability process in place to keep me on track?*

Hmmmmm... some tough questions here. Are your minimum standards high enough? Will they get you the success you desire? OR, is it time to raise your bar? **NO Excuses.**

Too Bad Tony

THE SHOW MUST GO ON... highly successful speaker/motivator Tony Robbins created a new TV show entitled "Breakthrough". It was to run for six segments on NBC. After the second show it was unceremoniously cancelled because of poor ratings! It was a pretty good show... it was about relationships. Apparently enough people didn't think so. Regardless, it was obvious that a tremendous amount of planning, effort, and staging was involved. In the end, **Tony was told he wasn't wanted...** end of story. Actually that's not true because Tony has a business to run. One setback didn't put him out of business. It's just that... one setback... nothing else. NEXT!

Here is your **ACTION STEP...** what happens when you receive that **"One Setback"?** How do you handle it when one of your Customer situations backfires... especially a big one, one that you were really counting on?

Rather than get caught up in the drama of disappointment here's a simple approach:

1. *Take a deep breath and accept the defeat.*

2. *Recognize that it is over and look forward, not back. Move on.*

3. *Remind yourself of your Big Picture... what are your Personal Goals?*

4. *Immerse yourself in positive activity. Get back to work.*

5. ***Critical Point:*** *rely on your DAILY ROUTINE to get you back on track. That's your "safe harbour". Forget about yesterday, it's already over.*

Remember this... *"there is a reason why the rear view mirror is so much smaller than the windshield".* Onward and upward... embrace the future. **NO Excuses.**

Chapter 7
Incredible Sales Skills

<u>Sales Killer #3</u>

GOT ANY CHANGE?... the next biggest Sales Killer, after Time Management and Complacency, is our **Resistance to Change**. Let me make it even simpler for you... our EGO gets in the way! *"I know what I'm doing, my way is just fine, it's always worked OK before, I'm pretty good this you know, etc... blah, blah, blah".* Think about it this way - Your EGO is what got you to your current level, but it is also what is keeping you there!

Here is your **ACTION STEP...** time to let go and take some risks! Start by identifying what would improve your Sales Results dramatically if you did it better;

1. *Energy level (eating healthier, more exercise, more sleep),*

2. *Time management (start by following your schedule exactly, especially in the AM... NO interruptions!),*

3. *Presentation skills (record yourself live & in colour and learn to be better),*

4. *Closing (close one more time than you are comfortable with, "I Laugh at Rejection"),*

5. *Daily accountability (consider hiring a Coach).*

Change will make you stronger, healthier, wealthier. It's about time, isn't it? **NO Excuses.**

Great Money Stories

PECUNIARY WISDOM... most people work hard. Better than that... most Salespeople work very hard! Great Salespeople are some of the hardest working people on the planet. It's sort of like being an entertainer or a professional athlete... *it looks easy until you try it.* The good news is that the Great Salespeople make lots of money. How to keep all that $$$? This Sales Tip is about making sure that all your hard work not only results in financial reward but that it **also results in financial success!**

Here is your **ACTION STEP...** here are five great "reads" to keep you ahead of the game financially:

1. ***The Richest Man in Babylon****... George S. Clason*

2. ***Secrets of the Millionaire Mind****... T. Harv Eker*

3. ***The Total Money Makeover****... Dave Ramsey*

4. ***Rich Dad Poor Dad****... Robert Kiyosaki*

5. ***The Wealthy Barber****... David Chilton*

If you have read all five of these... read them again. You already know how good they are. If you have not... then **go out and buy them all.** You are in for a real treat! As a group they are a collective roadmap to financial success. Your "$$$ GPS"! **NO Excuses.**

Sales Killer #8

I'm OK... Sales Killer #8 is **"Keeping your Skills in Neutral"**. Recently I had a Seminar attendee tell me that *"I've been selling for quite a while so my Selling Skills are fine... I'm OK in that regard"*. I was at a loss for words... not completely, but almost...LOL. Then it struck me... this may not be how most Salespeople **SAY** they think, but this is the way most Salespeople **ACT**. Top Salespeople never stop growing... whatever you are selling, never forget that you are in a VERY competitive business! Think about this question (it's confrontation time): How much time, effort, and energy do you put into "improving your skills" every day?

Here is your **ACTION STEP...** commit to ONE hour per day of personal development (don't fight this... you really can find the time if you decide it is important). Here are some ideas:

1. *Read for 30 minutes before you go to bed or early AM*

2. *Role play 30 minutes, 5 mornings per week*

3. *Go for a brisk walk 5-6 days a week*

4. *Hire a Coach!! How much is your procrastination costing you?*

5. *Listen to inspirational material every day*

6. *Watch powerful speakers on DVDs (slip in a comedy one sometimes)*

The Best salespeople are never standing still… if you are not growing, you are dying.

Be ALIVE!!! **NO Excuses.**

Winging It

THAT WAS NOT EASY... Grammy Night happens every February. You know them, the awards for popular musical achievement? The usual glitter and excess? At the same time, to get to that level... you have to be really, really good. One year we were all amazed watching "Pink" performing 100 feet above the crowd, dangling from a silk ribbon upside down and singing! And it was nothing short of incredible! If you saw it, you wouldn't soon forget it. So here's the redundant question: *"Do you think she had to practice that?"*

Here is your **ACTION STEP...** "Pink's" performance was so memorable was because it had 2 qualities:

1. *It was very high quality*
2. *It was very different*

Do you want your customers to remember you? Make sure every communication/presentation you make has the same two qualities. Your customers will only remember you if you *exhibit high quality and you are different.*

There's only one way to achieve that... PRACTICE, PRACTICE, PRACTICE. You will not win any awards (or sales) by being boringly forgettable. Commit today to putting the time in every day to being just 1% better. Pay the price and keep "sharpening your saw". **NO Excuses.**

Stand Out

UPPERCASE / LOWERCASE?... the recently departed comedian George Carlin was a master at finding humor in everyday situations. He said that there is a significant difference in the various letters of the alphabet. George reported that, *"UPPERCASE letters stand out... they are confident, they are noticeable, they are assumptive, they get what they want. LOWERCASE letters are hiding... they don't want attention, they just get by, they're almost afraid."* As humorous as all this is, there is definitely some wisdom here. As a Salesperson would your customers say you are an **UPPERCASE letter**... or a **LOWERCASE letter**?

Here is your **ACTION STEP...** done the right way, being UPPERCASE is better. You don't have to be a "noisy, obnoxious blow-hard" to achieve UPPERCASE status. Here are some great ideas on how to do it the right way:

1. *Dress smart and professionally* (not "look at me, look at me!")
2. *Know what you're going to say* (saying less usually "says more")
3. *Carry yourself confidently* (body language is critical)
4. *Smile, great eye contact, use their name* (just be "present")

5. *Practice asking LOTS OF QUESTIONS* (a great way to "be remembered")

Bonus Tip: just because you heard all this before, doesn't mean you are doing it to the level you can (or should). Being UPPERCASE is a lifelong project, enjoy your status. Would George Carlin notice you? **NO Excuses.**

Blinding Flash of the Obvious

THE LIGHT GOES ON!... While watching the British Open Golf Championship I was taken by an amazing sight. Four individuals were walking up the fairway towards the camera. It was raining and there really wasn't much of a crowd visible. Here's what I saw... at the rear of the pack was a fellow with a heavy television camera mounted on his shoulder. Beside him was a guy lugging a large sound boom and a whole bunch of cables. At the front was the caddy carrying a huge golf bag and an umbrella. At the front of the pack was the famous golfer... Phil Mickelson. And guess what?... He wasn't carrying anything!! What struck me was that everybody else was doing the "heavy lifting" and the Professional had the easiest job all. Why?... **Because He's the One with All the Skills!** What an amazing metaphor! A Blinding Flash of the Obvious. There is a direct connection between **No Heavy Lifting** and **Lots of Skills.**

Here is your ACTION STEP... in the Sales Business, it is your Skill set that sets you apart from the competition. It is our Skills that determine how much money we make. So if you want to make more money and do less "heavy lifting"... what are the skills that you should be working on every day? Here are some ideas:

1. *Consistent lead generation* *(1 2 3 4 5 6 7 8 9 10)*

2. Confident objection handling (1 2 3 4 5 6 7 8 9 10)

3. A powerful presentation (1 2 3 4 5 6 7 8 9 10)

4. Closing naturally (1 2 3 4 5 6 7 8 9 10)

5. Rock solid "mental toughness" (1 2 3 4 5 6 7 8 9 10)

Rate yourself on a scale of 1 to 10 for each of these items (10 being Superman/Superwoman). Be brutally honest. Now, starting with the most glaring deficiency... get to work at building that Skill. Really work at it! Ignore your fears and resistances. Shazam! The result will be... no more "heavy lifting". **NO Excuses.**

I Hate Scripts!

"TO SCRIPT OR NOT TO SCRIPT... that is the question?" (with apologies for the shameless twisting of William Shakespeare's famous line). Successful Salespeople use scripts on an ongoing basis. Some Salespeople deny that they use scripts, but everyone does. Just because it is not written down doesn't mean it's not a script. The most common resistance to using scripts is the following... *"I don't like using scripts because they sound canned and don't sound like me!".* There are two reasons for that... both of them valid:

1. You probably haven't practiced that script enough

2. You haven't changed some of the words so they will "sound like you"

Here is your **ACTION STEP...** think of this metaphor. Which vegetables do you think would be more healthy and more tasteful:

1. The vegetables you grow in your own garden?... OR...

2. The vegetables you buy in the store that have been in a cardboard box for who knows how long?

Obviously the answer is #1. So when it comes to scripts... **start growing your own vegetables!** Here is the formula:

1. Take a basic script that has a strong message that you like

2. Rewrite & internalize it using your language, your words, your comfort level

*3. Critical Point: you have now converted the original words into a **Conversation**...it's not a Script anymore!*

The key is the "rewrite & internalize" part. It's one thing to complain about a particular script and then keep saying what's in your head. It's a totally different (and much more professional) approach to rewrite it and have it on paper. Don't be lazy here... write them out! Now you can become the master of saying the right thing at the right time. You decide. Are you really committed to raising your craft to the next level? You already know that the "next level" pays a lot more. **NO Excuses.**

Being the BEST Presenter

IDOL WISDOM... in the 10th season of American Idol the producers brought in a permanent Coach for the contestants. They hired acclaimed music executive and record producer Jimmy Iovine (Chairman, Interscope-Geffen-A&M Records). What he does is help them **Improve on their Presentations.** Jimmy is very good at this... he offers amazing guidance and his critiques are excellent. Recently he casually offered some brilliant logic. Iovine said:

1. "When you are unsure of yourself, you lose confidence"

2. "When you lose confidence, everyone knows it!"

This "flash of insight" certainly applies to real life. We see both sides of that coin in many of the people we encounter on a day-to-day basis. It shows up in eye contact, lack of persistence, strength of a handshake, nervous habits, useless chatter, etc.

Here is your **ACTION STEP...** Note that all great Salespeople are **Sure of Themselves.** Your Customers are expecting this! Here are some great ways to position yourself powerfully for your Presentations:

1. *Start by looking good and feeling good... dress sharp, and give off lots of great energy.*

2. *Make sure that you have a structured presentation. Have a plan for how you are going to perform.*

3. *Know exactly what you're going to say. This starts with a script.*

4. *Practice your delivery before you present. This builds confidence.*

5. *Show them exactly how you are going to help them get what they want.*

Follow the above formula. Look at the logical progression in Jimmy Iovine's wisdom… *"when you are sure of yourself, you are confident… when you are confident everyone knows it! When everyone knows it, they will buy what you are offering".* Be prepared, be the professional, be the Winner you know you can be. **NO Excuses.**

Prize Winning Chef

BAKE THAT CAKE... there are certain things that can only be done one way. Those who are magnificent at baking tell us that there is really only one way to get the job done. You must *"follow the recipe that the experts have created... don't change what works".* In talking to someone who is a great Baker of Cakes (my wife Gloria) I have learned that every time they play with the recipe... or they forget an ingredient... **the cake falls flat!** Are you guilty of *" changing the recipe sometimes?".*

Here is your **ACTION STEP...** the most common example of Salespeople *"changing the recipe"* is in the use of scripts. Scripts are designed to get the job done faster and more professionally, using fewer words. Here are some of the excuses I hear for not using scripts:

1. *"I don't want to sound canned."* (Realize everything sounds "canned" until you practice it)

2. *"I hate practicing!."* (Professionals practice – Amateurs make excuses)

3. *"These are not my words."* (They just might be better words! Have an open mind.)

A TRUISM: the only reason people resist using scripts is that their EGO gets in the way. There is good ego and there is bad ego. Bad Ego is when you get in the way of self-improvement.

Be Coachable here... people on Broadway and in the movies do not "wing it". Otherwise their performance will invariably "fall flat"!

From now on, start USING SCRIPTS... don't let your performance suffer. Bake that prize-winning cake every time. **NO Excuses.**

Help Others and Help You

ROLE-PLAYING RESISTANCE... one of the most effective ways to become a great Salesperson is to become a great Communicator. The most effective way to become a great communicator is to practice... to role-play with others. There is a tremendous amount of resistance to role-playing. Just remember this... **get comfortable with role-playing and you can also get comfortable with "a fat bank account". There is a connection.** Here is the secret: the best way to get comfortable with role-playing is to become a very effective role-play partner. By becoming someone that "everyone wants to practice with"... you automatically are going to become a great communicator (ergo – Salesperson). It's a guaranteed side benefit.

Here is your **ACTION STEP...** there are two ways to become a great role-play partner. First, you must be very reliable, which means you must show up on time every time. Second, you must become adept at giving a powerful and insightful critique. Help others and you will get better really fast! Here is a simple list of the things you should look for when you are offering your "great critique":

1. *Energy level*

2. *Rate of speech*

3. *Tonality – voice upswings, downswings, etc.*

4. *Expressiveness – enthusiasm*

5. Confidence level

6. Ease of delivery – "conversationalism"

7. Number of closes

8. Sticking to the script

9. Listening skills

Keep this list handy when you are critiquing your partner. Remember to point out things they are doing well in addition to offering "constructive criticism". Don't be negative, be encouraging! Encouragement is part of a powerful critique. Make role-playing fun and you will make a lot more money. **NO Excuses.**

Chapter 8
The Mindset of a Winner

The "Un-Fab" Four

FOUR "KILLER" WORDS... there are four dangerous words that I hear all the time... usually from Salespeople who are unconsciously planning to fail. They are... **"YEAH BUT"** & **"AT LEAST".** They show up like this:

1. YEAH BUT... "yeah but that wouldn't work for me / yeah but I could never say that / yeah but I haven't got the time / etc., etc., etc."

2. AT LEAST... "at least I am doing some of the things I should / at least it's better than doing nothing / at least I tried to do it / etc., etc., etc."

These are just well disguised excuses, in an attempt to give yourself permission to fail. It's like you are giving yourself an 'escape hatch'.

Here is your **ACTION STEP...** next time you hear yourself even hinting at using those four words... *give yourself a slap!!* **Take them out of your vocabulary.** Take responsibility for doing exactly what you said you would. Commit to this approach, *"Not doing it is NOT an option".*

Be the Superstar you said you were going to be when you did your annual business plan... and be the Superstar you are capable of being. Every day! The alternative is just not acceptable, is it? **NO Excuses.**

What You Believe

MOVIE WISDOM… a movie entitled *"Deception"* was released in 2008. It's a suspense melodrama with an entertaining ending, starring Hugh Jackman. It highlights how sometimes we are the beneficiaries of great advice when we least expect it. In the movie script, Jackman's character delivered the following line… *"He believed he would never scale that wall and the truth is, he was the only one guarding it!"* It was one of those AHA moments where I had to put the movie on pause and tell myself "write that one down, Bruce". How many times do we **"believe we can't scale that wall"** when nothing is stopping us?

Here is your **ACTION STEP…** success in business, success in sales, and success in life is 90% predicated by what we believe. As Henry Ford said, *"if you believe you can… or believe you can't… either way you are right".* Here are some great ideas on how to develop a strong belief in yourself:

1. *Physiology is first… carry yourself with confidence and pride. This is critical.*

2. *Self-confidence is next… start by being your word for everything you commit to. Hold yourself accountable. Not doing what you say is not an option!*

3. *Focus on Action: identify the task and create small steps to achieve it. Minimize the thinking part. Like NIKE: "Just do it".*

4. *Surround yourself with people who support you. Tell them what you are about to do. They want you to succeed.*

5. *Expect "bumps in the road"... go over, under, or around them... never give up. Persevere ("be your word"). Mental Toughness is so important.*

6. *Celebrate every one of your victories, small and large... you do not need an excuse to feel good! Recognize that every victory is a HUGE step forward. Congratulations!*

BONUS TIP: remember that great observation from author Chad Helmstetter... *"Fully 95% of our emotions* (and therefore our beliefs) *are controlled by how we talk to ourselves".* Be a "vicious guard dog" at the door of your mind. Your beliefs will allow you to achieve everything you ever wanted! **NO Excuses.**

Sales Killer #9

INTEGRITY... Sales Killer #9 is **Not Being Your Word.** If asked to rate themselves on a scale of 1-10 for honesty & integrity, most Salespeople would rate themselves a 9 or a 10. *"I don't lie, cheat, or steal... that's not who I am!"* The problem is that while you might not lie to others, sometimes you lie to yourself.

Here's what I've learned as a Speaker and Coach over the last 14+ years... *people are much* more *honest with everyone else than they are with themselves! You say you're going to do things and then you "break your word to yourself"...* sometimes repeatedly. The question then becomes, *"Why do you treat everyone else with more respect than you treat yourself?".*

Hmmmm, think about that one. (Read that question twice!)

Here is your **ACTION PLAN...** there is a very simple solution here... **be much more selective about what you agree to do**. Here is a formula that really helps:

1. *Before you agree to do something... be sure you are committed*

2. *If you are committed then make sure you have time to actually do it*

3. *Keep track of how much you are taking on, there is a limit!!*

4. *Be Your Word... let absolutely nothing erode your integrity*

Last thought... your Integrity defines who you are. Be as honest with yourself as you are with everyone else. **Personal Integrity** is a critical component of Self-Confidence. **NO Excuses.**

HELP!

STARRING ROLE... it's not hard to imagine your life as a movie. No successful sales career is without *"bumps in the road"* You know, those challenges that always seem to be popping up just when you do not need them. The real issue is not the *"bumps"* but... how well do we navigate through them. You can a) drive over them; or b) drive around them; or c) stop the car, get out and make a full-length miniseries about your troubles. Those who choose option c) always seem to have a reason for saying, *"You don't understand... this is different".* Some people are addicted to creating drama for everything in their life. WHY?... because it draws attention to them! If ever you are guilty - break that habit fast!

HOW? Here is your **ACTION STEP...** we all need to accept this wisdom: **"Sooner or later we all discover that NO ONE is coming to the rescue!"** In other words, *"if it's to be then it is up to me"...* When that *"bump"* pops up (big or small) here's what you do:

1. *Take a deep breath and write down your options*
2. *Pick the best one without creating a scene*
3. *Write out the Action Steps needed to "get it done"*
4. *Take action! (avoid the drama... remember, "no one is coming to the rescue")*

PS... most people are guilty of this sometimes. At least make it a "short subject" movie when you find yourself in a starring role. **NO Excuses.**

JINXED?

BAD LUCK... one of my Coaching Clients recently pointed out that he'd had a particularly tough run of "bad luck". The question then became, *"Bruce, how do I get it to end?!!!".* Before I answer that question, let's be honest... the Selling Process seldom runs smoothly. Your results never arrive the way you expect them to. You will run into stretches where *"nothing seems to go right".* So, you have to learn how to deal with it, right?

Here is your **ACTION STEP...** whenever you feel that you are having bad luck, remember the following:

1. *There is no such thing as "bad luck"... or "good luck", for that matter*

2. *The Law of Attraction will work against you if you are feeling low... use a "pattern interrupt" to snap yourself out of it (e.g.: say "STOP IT, STOP IT, STOP IT, out loud, 3 times)*

3. *Get "back on the horse" immediately... fill up your conveyor belt with lots of good activity. It will shorten the cycle.*

Affirmation: *"I allow no slump to last more than 24 hours!!"* **NO Excuses.**

PS... that Coaching Client with all the "bad luck" went out the next day and set 2 appointments. **YES!!**

My Way

DON'T LOOK BACK... Paul Anka's beautiful song "My Way" was crooned by Frank Sinatra so poignantly. Remember these words?...

"Regrets, I've had a few... but then again, too few to mention".

Do you spend any time worrying about what could have been... things that went in the wrong direction? Probably, most people do. My advice to you is to...Let it go! The fact is those things are in the past. Regardless, the good news is... they are probably "too few to mention" anyway.

Here is your **ACTION STEP...** and here's the best part... all that stuff is behind you. It is a new day!! Whatever happened before is of no significance. TODAY, you are free to create new results, new successes. Superstars dwell on what "can be".

Here's a great quote to remind you to always MOVE FORWARD:

"There is a reason why the windshield is so much larger than the rearview mirror...!!!"

Let's say you are halfway through your business year. What has taken place is already over, but more importantly what is going to happen is still ahead of you.

Here's what to do: Look at your business plan, look at your activities, make the necessary adjustments and move forward! Your future is a blank cheque… you are in charge. Follow Paul Anka's advice – do it "My Way".. **NO Excuses.**

Isn't That Strange?

MAKES ME THINK... recently we looked at some great "puzzlers" from NCAA Coaching legend John Wooden. John always had a knack for asking great questions that made us think. We all have our own personal puzzlers. After 40+ continuous years in Sales, I have some puzzlers too.

Here are some **"BK Puzzlers"...** things that make me wonder......:

1. Why is it that so many Salespeople have trouble making the connection between their activities and their goals?

2. Isn't it strange that professional entertainers and athletes practice a lot and Salespeople don't? Who makes more $$$?

3. Why is it that people who do not like their results keep doing the same things over and over without changing?

4. Isn't it curious that cheerful people are always being criticized for being out of touch with reality?

5. What is it about the news on television that's so interesting? (Answer... 'Not much')

Here is your **ACTION STEP...** ask yourself...

1. *How many of these 5 BK Puzzlers apply to you? Have a look and be honest with yourself.*

2. *What adjustments could you make?*

NO Excuses.

Need Help Staying on Schedule?

THE SUCCESS CORNER... by far the biggest challenge in Selling is to generate consistent results. The best way to do that of course is to Stick to Your Schedule. There is an old adage in life about being careful not to *"paint yourself into a corner".* The implication is that once you have done that... you are stuck and can't get out. **What if you looked at it another way: what if the corner you painted yourself into was a "Success Corner"?** What if you set up your day so that you had no alternative but to STAY ON SCHEDULE?

Here is your **ACTION STEP...** the first step is to have a firm Daily Schedule. The next step is to follow it every day. *"So how do I do that, Bruce?",* you ask. Here are some of my Top Time Management Tips:

1. *Prepare for the next day... the night before*
2. *Critical Point #1: get up at the same time every morning (regardless what time you went to bed!)*
3. *Do the most difficult tasks first. Get them out of the way before the "Excuse Buffet" arrives.*
4. *Critical Point #2: eliminate all options... say NO to every possible interruption.*
5. *Commit to Growth and Accountability... get someone to hold your "feet to the fire" (how about an experienced Coach with proven results?)*

If you are truly committed to *"painting yourself into a Success Corner"* then pay special attention to #5 above. **This is the one that makes everything work. NO Excuses.**

How Top Performers Act

LADY GAGA... is hard to miss. A Songstress, Composer and stage Performer, she's very entertaining... and she's everywhere! Many of the things she does are outlandish and certainly attract a lot of attention. Regardless, for her to be that successful and always at the top of her game **certainly does not come without a lot of mental toughness.** Recently Lady Gaga was asked how it felt to be so famous? Her answer displayed a lot of wisdom. She said, *"I knew I was famous before anyone else did."* It was as simple as that... the old *"fake it until you make it"* approach.

Here is your **ACTION STEP...** in other words your success should never come as a surprise to you! One of the ways to *"get there"* is to act as if *"I'm already there"*. Here are some ideas on how to do that:

1. ***Dress** the part of "the person who you intend to be" every day. Even if you only have one outfit... look sharp every day.*

2. ***Act** the part every day. Believe in yourself. Conduct yourself like the Superstar Salesperson you are.*

3. ***Stand tall**, exhibit strong energy... people are attracted to energy!*

4. ***Treat** everyone like your Best Customer... everyone ... including the greeter at Wal-Mart. Be easy to like.*

5. ***Be happy!*** *Laugh out loud five times every day. Listen to or watch some comedy material daily.*

Be proud of who you are, be inspired, and make others want to be around you. Here's a great affirmation for you... *"I'm Already There!".* Say that one out loud <u>five times</u> every morning. **NO Excuses.**

I Deserve…

ENTITLEMENT… there is a sense in our North American culture that says once we earn something we deserve that reputation forever. Some people feel that they are "entitled" to whatever they want, whenever they want it. It's that *"I have arrived"* mindset. From the outside looking in, those individuals seem tremendously "full of themselves"… EGO out-of-control. In his recent publication called ***Entitlement,*** Author Brad Hams explains that those who feel *"continuously deserving… typically do not receive rewards equal to their expectations".* Why not? Because the truth is that we only get rewarded for what we do today. Entitlement has a "short shelf-life".

Here is your **ACTION STEP…** the top Salespeople never forget the mantra, **"I Start Every Day at Zero".** Here's a great way to keep your EGO where it belongs:

1. *Forget about yesterday, it doesn't mean anything now*

2. *Ask yourself, "What must I accomplish today to be satisfied tonight?"*

3. *Forget about the "you owe me" mentality. Earn your way every day*

4. *Take responsibility for "Starting Every Day at Zero"*

The only way to stay successful is to earn it every day. The real paradox is that those great Salespeople who really are entitled to success are the very same ones who **go out and earn it every single day.** Entitlement is not in their thinking. The alternative is complacency! Not Acceptable. **NO Excuses.**

Chapter 9
Reality Checks

One Word: WOW!

ARE THEY AMAZING or WHAT?... the Paralympics are held every 4 years. Next to the traditional Olympics, the Paralympics is the biggest single amateur sporting event in the world! Pretty amazing, considering it only officially it began in 1992. It showcases people from all walks of life and a multitude of nations, spanning the globe. These are accomplished athletes **who are really good at overcoming adversity and ignoring their handicaps.** You know where I'm going here...

Here is your **ACTION STEP... ask yourself, REALLY ...**

1. *How severe is the adversity you face?*
2. *How significant is the handicap that is holding you back?*

Realize that we are all confronted with "bumps in the road". Some are big, and some not so big. We all have our stories.

Regardless, here's what sets us apart... How well do you step up and say, *"This is my opportunity to be better than the rest. This is my opportunity to use my Mental Toughness and over-achieve".?*

Take advantage of all your "bumps", they are there to test you. It's your chance to stand out. Grab it and run!! **NO Excuses.**

Beware the December Slippery Slope

AVOID OVERINDULGENCE... For most people, December is good news / bad news. The most festive month of the year is a real test of our self-discipline. We are continually presented with the temptation of *eating too much of the wrong thing!* Saying NO is hard sometimes... especially when it comes to "all those treats"! Great Salespeople have great energy. If your energy suffers, so will your bank account... it is that simple.

Here is your ACTION STEP:

1. *Set a maximum weight that you will not go above in December*

2. *For this month only... weigh yourself every day*

3. *Be conscious of the huge impact that sugar & fat has on your energy*

4. *Stop telling yourself, "I have earned this extra cookie" etc...* ***you haven't earned poor health!***

5. *Take pride in your ability to Enjoy but do not Overindulge*

Look after yourself 12 months a year. Don't sabotage all the effort you have put into being healthy in just one month. Your energy is your biggest asset as a Salesperson. **NO Excuses.**

Sales Killer #4

GET REAL... Sales Killer #4 is "Not being Realistic". A long time ago I learned that there is a simple equation to winning the Sales Game. Are you ready? Here goes...it's very basic...

A = G

(your **A**ctivities must be in line with your **G**oals)

That's it... so if you're not reaching your Goals then it is because you are not doing enough of the Activities that it takes to get you there.

Here's your **ACTION PLAN...** your Activities must be in concert with your Goals/targets:

1. *Revisit your goals/sales targets. Make sure they will get you where you want to go*
2. ***Critical:** calculate what activities are needed to achieve that and result (eg: one new sale per week)*
3. *Decide how many DAILY contacts are necessary for that to happen (be realistic... what's it going to take?)*
4. *Make sure that amount of prospecting is in your schedule as your Top Priority*
5. *Eliminate all the reasons why you can't* ... AND START TODAY!

Remember, your Goals and your Activities must match up exactly. **NO Excuses.**

Curious George

LOSING NOT ALLOWED... George Steinbrenner passed away in 2010, at the age of 80. George's main claim to fame was his highly successful ownership and management of the New York Yankees baseball team. It's arguably the most well-known sports franchise in the world. Love him or hate him, George Steinbrenner was an amazing man. He also had a reputation for being cantankerous. This was popularized very successfully on TV's "Seinfeld" when he was portrayed as George Costanza's boss with the Yankees. One of his most famous quotes was, *"I do not like to lose. Show me a Good Loser and I will still show you a Loser!"* There is certainly some great wisdom in this arrogance.

Here is your ACTION STEP... what George was saying is that if you say *"It's Okay to Lose"* then you really are opening the door for a lot of disappointment. *So let's turn this around... and ask ...how do Winners operate?*

Here's the list:

BK's Winner's Characteristics

1. They expect to win every time.
2. They keep score consistently.
3. They practice more than they perform.
4. They have a Coach (for skills and accountability).
5. They never give up.

I suspect you are already aware of the above list Winner's Characteristics. The real question is... do you actually operate that way?!! Step back and evaluate yourself. Are you operating like a Winner? **NO Excuses.**

The Dream World

THAT WAS EASY... we've all had fun at the Staples store pushing the big red "Easy" button and hearing it say the magic words... *"That was easy".* It's a great marketing tool and no doubt it has served Staples very well. The truth is, as we all know, the real world isn't quite that "easy". We can all dream about winning the lottery... but the truth is there are really are not any Short Cuts, are there? As a matter of fact, we are much better to operate under the credo that says, ***"if it seems too good to be true it probably is".***

Here is your **ACTION STEP...** lots of people are in a Dreamworld ... *DON'T you be one of them*!

Too many people keep looking for the magic pill. The chances of an easy sale are small and by waiting for that to happen you greatly diminish your ability to do the REAL WORK. It's fun to dream, but the fact is that (and the sooner you learn this the better off you'll be):

1. *Oprah is probably not going to endorse your book*
2. *It is unlikely that you will ever win the lottery*
3. *Warren Buffett isn't going to call*
4. *That hot "stock tip" isn't all that hot*
5. *No one is "coming to the rescue"*

Great Salespeople do the REAL WORK every day, all days... day in and day out. When you try to find an easy way, when you try to cut corners, when you look for shortcuts... **you get burned.**

So do yourself a favour, do your job every day and periodically something fortuitous will come your way. And when it does… you will have earned it… not because you 'got lucky'! **NO Excuses.**

Bob Proctor Makes Sense Here

REPETITION... every time we watch a professional perform we are struck by "how easy it looks". Whether it is a professional athlete or an entertainer, it is very clear that there has been a lot of practice involved. As the joke goes... *"I guess that's not the first time they have done that".* The other day I was listening to professional motivator/speaker Bob Proctor. He casually mentioned that *"Repetition is the 1st Law of Learning".* I pressed "pause" and thought about that. As usual some of the simplest statements are the most profound!

Here is your **ACTION STEP...** if *"Repetition Is the 1st Law of Learning"* then let's look at some of the things we need to do on a REPETITIVE BASIS. That way you will get better and better just by doing them more frequently:

1. *Listening more / talking less, by **asking more questions***

2. *Following a **Daily Routine** that becomes powerfully habitual*

3. ***Scheduling time off to** refresh your Business Energy*

4. *Associating with **Inspiring People** (example: take someone special to lunch next week)*

5. ***Practicing what you say** (scripts) instead of the "improv" approach*

Take Bob Proctor's advice... Do the right things over and over ... Practice Repetition. Which of the above items do you need to do more often? Start with one today. The by-product of all this is an ever-increasing Level of Self-Confidence. Take yourself to that Next Level. **NO Excuses.**

4 Steps to "Get'er Done"

FAULTY EXIT STRATEGY... in his book about relationships, Dr. Harville Hendrix does a great job of explaining *"how creative we are in avoiding the things we do not want to do".* He says **we create "EXITS".** These Exits take the form of alternative tasks... *"stuff I just gotta do right now".* People become very innovative in their avoidance. Here's the worst part... most of the time, the tasks that you let interrupt you are not nearly as important as the ones you are avoiding! Dr. Hendrix goes on to say, these **Exits are just another form of EXCUSES.** So what Exits are habitual in your life and your business?

Here is your **ACTION STEP...** the first thing to recognize is that there may just be some negative habits (i.e.: Exits) that are getting in the way of your success. Once you have accepted that... here are some simple ideas on how to move forward:

1. *Identify the three or four CRITICAL tasks **you must accomplish everyday***

2. *List the repetitive Exits that you use that unconsciously sabotage you*

3. *Think about the "fear factor" that is preventing you from doing those CRITICAL tasks. What is the worst that could happen? Usually the answer is... Not Much!*

4. ***Select two Exits*** *which would be the easiest for you to eliminate, immediately*

5. *Be merciless with them... the next time they appear, ignore them entirely!*

Most people know when an Exit is an avoidance or excuse. Be brutally honest with yourself. Over time you will eliminate them all. And from now on... **NO Excuses.**

Painful Lessons

SO CLOSE!... On Thursday, November 24, 2011 the Texas Rangers were one strike away from winning their very first World Series championship, after over 50 years of trying. As a matter of fact they were one strike away from winning... on two occasions! It first happened in the bottom of the 9th inning but the St. Louis Cardinals tied the game. It also happened in the bottom of the 10th inning and the pesky Cards got off the hook one more time. The end result?... St. Louis won the sixth game in the bottom of the 11th and went on to win the World Series in Game Seven one night later. **Close, but no cigar!** Imagine how the players from the Texas Rangers felt after that turn of events. We have all lost out in situations where it looked like we were going to be victorious. It doesn't feel very good... and sometimes it is devastating!

As always, once you get over your initial disappointment... **know that there are lessons to be learned. Here are four of them, as they pertains to Sales:**

1. *In Sales, as in baseball... there are no sure things. When you are in sight of victory, don't let up. Close one more time and stay focused on the prize you are pursuing. Never "take your eye off the ball", especially when you are so close.*

2. *Never give up. Until you get your final NO... keep pressing. Keep asking for the order, keep smiling, keep your emotions in check, and keep presenting*

the benefits of choosing you, your product, and your services.

3. *Accept the fact that sometimes no matter what you do... victory may not be yours. There are other competitors out there who are also very good. At the same time, always operate under the assumption that you are the best. Why not?*

4. *There is always another game. There is always another Customer to call on and there is always another Sale to make. One loss... no matter how devastating... is just that. It is only one loss. Just say NEXT! Go out and find your next opportunity... take comfort from the fact that you are now that much closer to a YES.*

These lessons are there for everyone. Of course they are easier to accept when they happen to someone else. No doubt the Texas Rangers got up the next morning, dusted themselves off, and got on with life. Some of the players no doubt handled it better than others, some of them took longer to "get over it". In the big picture, the truth is "it's only baseball"... Life is what you make it. In the Sales picture, the truth is "it's only Sales". Your life is what you make it. There are a lot more important things in life. Sometimes you just need to be philosophical and count your blessings.

Here is your **ACTION STEP** ... *Why not take 60 seconds and do that right now?*

It feels good. **NO Excuses.**

Making Powerful Connections

CONNECTING THE DOTS... there are some very clear Connections in life that never prompt debate. There are certain truths that we all accept and use to help us make decisions. One of the most common Connections is the relationship between proper FOOD and good HEALTH. Everybody knows that good food is a major component in contributing to good health. It's a very logical Connection.

Here is your **ACTION STEP...** there are a lot of powerful Connections In Selling. These are truths that help us become dramatically more successful. *Here are a few to ponder:*

BK's Connections in Sales

1. A positive attitude and the ability to "bounce back"

2. The size of your database and the number of referrals

3. The number of contacts made and the number of sales

4. The hours practiced and your level of confidence

5. The number of closes and the number of "YES's"

6. Professional dress and successful presentations

7. Your physiology and customer rapport (think about this one... very powerful)

8. Persistent follow-up and results achieved

9. The frequency of exercise and amount of energy

There are plenty more, I'm sure. Have a look at this list and decide **what you can do to become an even better Salesperson**. Take yourself to the next level... growing is fun (oops, there's another one... *your ability to change and amount you grow!*). **NO Excuses.**

7 Simple Success Nuggets

SELF-SABOTAGE... some people often get in their own way and sabotage themselves. A lot of Salespeople lose out on business simply because they do not Ask for It! As ridiculous as this may sound, sometimes we are all guilty of missing opportunities. We say things to ourselves like, *"They know what I do for a living... if they need me they will call me".* As the joke goes: we become "Secret Agents". In my Seminars and Coaching this appears quite frequently. When asked, the guilty parties often confess that they are *"avoiding rejection / being forgetful / or are not sure what to say".* This is just one example of how some Salespeople sabotage their success.

Here is your **ACTION STEP...** one proven path to being a Superstar is to eliminate your shortfalls. Let's look at a list of some other self-sabotaging techniques that the less successful Salespeople commit ... and these are things that you should not do:

1. *They arrive at the office late*
2. *They don't practice*
3. *They don't keep their Past Client/Center of Influence database current*
4. *They don't ask their Past Client/Center of Influence for business or referrals*
5. *They don't prospect for business every day*

6. *They don't follow up the leads they already have*

7. *They don't ask for business at every opportunity*

8. *They don't have a "sense of urgency" in their life*

I know you're not guilty of all of the above. Let's do a "Be Honest" here... **pick out two or three items that you know you should improve on.** Tackle those right away. Superstars are always improving! **NO Excuses.**

Chapter 10
Staying Motivated

Is This a Bit Like You?

ADDICTED TO APPROVAL... in a recent TV interview with Dr. Phil, it was revealed that Sarah Ferguson (ex-wife of England's Prince Andrew) is "addicted to approval/addicted to acceptance". She has proven, rather unfortunately, in the past that she will do anything to get approval. So much so that as Dr. Phil pointed out to her... ***"You will even put yourself in harm's way to get that all-important approval!".*** I am not suggesting to you that you necessarily suffer the same affliction... at least not to that degree. At the same time, I do see a lot of Salespeople who do some things that are certainly imprudent when it comes to building a successful Sales Career. Foolish things... all because they are trying to make their Customer really like them... going overboard to be accepted by that Customer.

Here is your **ACTION STEP...** are you "Addicted to Approval"? How many of the following situations are true for you? Do you often work with Customers who...

1. *Are not motivated to buy in the reasonable future?*
2. *Are abusive and treat you with disrespect?*
3. *Expect to hear back from you 24 hours/day, regardless when they call?*
4. *Make unrealistic demands on your time and your capabilities?*
5. *Are unrealistic in their expectations of what they can buy for their budget?*
6. *Expect you to work for very little commission?*

7. *Critical Point: Don't make you feel very good about yourself?*

If the answer is YES to some or any of these it is time to step up to it! You wouldn't hang around someone who has a communicable disease for very long, would you? These Customers will infect your mind! **The SOLUTION?...** The first thing to do is to give yourself a big "hug" and say "NO MORE". Next would be to realize you deserve better. Then, after you eliminate those people from your life (fast)... start prospecting for good Customers. Look for people who need you and respect you - they are definitely out there. Spot the signs within yourself of "needing constant approval" and move away from compromising your feelings. Keep yourself "out of harm's way". **NO Excuses.**

Best Five Classics

SERIOUS BUSINESS... successful selling is a serious business, and yet it doesn't mean you can't have a good time while succeeding. Great Salespeople LOVE what they do and have a great time doing it. As you've heard me say before... *"It's only real estate; or it's only insurance, or computers, or investments, whatever"!!!* Don't make a BIG deal out of it. Bottom line is we all need to laugh more. Why?... because it'll help you be more successful.

Here's your ACTION PLAN... go out today and buy two (not one) of the following great comedy DVDs. (I have personally reviewed dozens to get this list down to **BK's Top Five Comedy Classics)...**

1. John Pinette -*"I'm Starving"*
2. Russell Peters -*"Outsourced"*
3. Jerry Seinfeld -*"Live on Broadway"*
4. Steven Wright -*"When the Leaves Blow Away"*
5. Brian Regan -*"The Epitome of Hyperbole"*

Remember... invest in two, not one... pop them in right away ... and start laughing more. A happy Salesperson creates happy customers. **NO Excuses.**

When's Your Next Snow Day?

SNOW DAY... growing up in 'the frozen north' it was always a treat to get a day off school because it was a Snow Day. It meant since the buses couldn't run due to a huge dump of snow school was cancelled. It usually happened 3-4 times every winter, and it was always a great surprise. We all should have the odd Snow Day... don't you think? All great Salespeople deserve a break.

Here is your ACTION STEP... *decide to take one day per month, and call it your own personal SNOW DAY !!!* (no more, no less... just once a month, okay?).

It works best to do it spontaneously... spur of the moment, just like waking up to a snow storm. Work hard the rest of the time so you can really appreciate the reward.

On your Snow Day, go shopping, go to a Spa, rent 4 movies, disappear for the day, have a fancy lunch... reward yourself!!! Do it once per month and make it fun. You will sell more and you'll work more effectively because **"there's another Snow Day just around the corner!". NO Excuses.**

R.V.F.S.

NEW ACRONYM... today's Sales Tip is all about breaking your routine. Why do we take vacations? Why do we go on long, elaborate trips? One main reason is because those are the fun and special times for ourselves and our family. That's how we create the valuable memories that last forever. For that matter, they don't even have to be long and elaborate... they just have to be different from our normal routine. There is another reason we take vacations... new acronym:

R.V.F.S.... Renewed Vigour For Success... it is healthy to "get away", to eliminate the ongoing stress in our everyday lives. You will go away and come back 10 years younger!!!

Here is your **ACTION STEP...** great Salespeople follow a solid daily/weekly routine. The real value in that routine is giving yourself permission to periodically interrupt it in spectacular fashion!!! Follow this approach:

1. *Pick something really exciting that you want to do in the next 6 months*

2. *Set a date AND book it (pay a deposit & no cancellations allowed)*

3. *Put it in your calendar, and announce your plans to the world!*

4. *Post some pictures to remind you everyday*

5. *Stick to your daily routine and count down the days... GET PUMPED!!*

6. *Go away and return with an* ***RVFS.... Renewed Vigour For Success!!***

Bonus Tip: Two great books to get you started are ***Unforgettable Places to See Before You Die*** by Steve Davey, and ***Unforgettable Things to do Before You Die*** *by* Watkins and Jones.

Have fun! **NO Excuses.**

March Break

SEVEN to NINE DAYS... Every once in a while you need to take a planned break. A time for some rest & relief from the daily highs & lows of Sales. These breaks are critical to maintaining a strong mindset. It's what the psychologists refer to as "refreshing your mind". This is critical... be sure you take time to do it. A problem comes with this time off however... the question is, *for how long do we really stop working? Is it just the planned 7-9 days or does it become nearly two weeks?*

Here is your **ACTION STEP...** there's really 3 issues to be strong about:

1. *Plan the time off and know exactly when it starts & stops*
2. *Work right up to "break time"... no slowing down early!*
3. *Come back with everything ready to get right back at it... restart fast, stay in momentum*

Take the time off, you have earned it... just be sure to "put a fence around it". Make sure there is no "gray area" related to #1 above. **NO Excuses.**

Mad Men – Season #4

OVERWHELM IS A KILLER... The Business of Sales has a tremendous amount of appeal because of the leverage it provides for our time and our income. Many people get into the Sales Game because of the freedom it allows in their day-to-day activities. The thought of not having a 9 to 5 day is very appealing (except on the occasion you work three nights in a row). The second "carrot" for being in Sales is the fact that you can earn as much money as you want... you have direct control of your income. Of course there are always two sides to the story and sometimes we get OVERWHELMED. We work too hard and nothing seems to go right... the pressure builds up and we feel like we are ready to explode! In a recent episode of the Emmy winning show, "MAD MEN – Season #4", overwhelm overtook main character Don Draper. He was exhausted and was behaving irrationally. He was easily irritated. One of his member Senior Partners offered an excellent and very wise solution...

Here is your **ACTION STEP...** the advice Don got went like this... *"When I am out of sorts, I always look at the calendar – there is usually something significant in there".* Great Advice! One of the best antidotes for Overwhelm is a reminder of two things:

1. *Why am I doing this work?*

2. *What do I have to look forward to?*

Take this approach:

1. *Put a big calendar on the wall. Preferably a "Year at a Glance" model. (See my YouTube video entitled "Time Management Board")*

2. *Schedule and mark down some exciting things in your future (trips, vacations, activities, etc.)*

3. *Focus on looking forward to the things you are going to do*

Don't let Overwhelm be front and center... you deserve better! Look at it this way... sometimes the price seems fairly high. At the same time here's a great question to ask yourself... *"What's the alternative?"*. Usually the alternative is less appealing than all the exciting things you have planned for your future. Work on your skills, stay focused, and remind yourself of why you are doing the things you are doing. **Keep your rewards highly visible!** It's usually worth it! **NO Excuses.**

One in the Same

HEALTHY BODY / HEALTHY MIND... I encourage you to pick up a copy of SUCCESS Magazine every month. It is always full of great articles on how to overachieve. It also includes a free "Success CD" in every edition. The CD itself is worth the cost because it contains a series of interviews one-on-one with some great minds. The May 2010 publication was all about Personal Fitness and its related benefits. One of those interviewed is fitness expert Chris Guerriero. Publisher Darren Hardy asked him, *"Which is more important... a Healthy Body or a Healthy Mind?"*.

Here is your **ACTION STEP...** Mr. Guerriero had a very interesting answer. He said... *"A healthy body & a healthy mind are not possible without each other. They are interdependent."*

How does this relate to selling? We all know that Success is Selling 90% Mindset. So here's the bottom line... **Mental toughness is a critical ingredient to Selling success.** If you are not physically fit then you cannot expect to be mentally tough. Here's what to do:

1. *Accept that you need to exercise regularly*

2. *Immediately put this in your routine*

3. *Here's the bad news... you must do it for the rest of your life!*

4. *Here's the good news... the "rest of your life" will last longer!*
5. *With a healthier body you will have amazing energy, you'll fight off rejection easier, you will attract success, and your results will be astounding.* ***JUST DO IT.***

'Nuff Said... this is quite possibly the most important Sales Tip of all!

Please read it again... just for you. **NO Excuses.**

Who's the Boss?

REPORTING STRUCTURE... traditional business operates under a well-defined reporting structure. Fred reports to Bob, who reports to Martha, etc. etc. etc. The fact is nowadays traditional business isn't traditional anymore! Many professions do not really have a reporting structure. The advent of the Independent Contractor has changed all that. People want to be entrepreneurial... to be "my own boss". Being your own boss allows you to do whatever you want, whenever you want. This allows for innovation and rapid growth. Of course with any change there are downsides too. When no one is holding you accountable it is much easier to lose your drive, your desire to succeed, even your motivation!

Here is you **ACTION STEP...** when you become your own boss you also take on the responsibility of "Being Your Own Sales Manager". Sales Managers are supposed to motivate their Salespeople. Sales Managers are supposed to inspire their Salespeople and hold them accountable. If you are your own Sales Manager... how do you stay focused and on track? Here are some questions to help you:

1. *Is it time to revise your personal goals? How current are they?*

2. *Do you have a project in your personal life that inspires you?*

3. *Do you look in the mirror and feel excited about who you see?*

4. *Who is your mentor? Who inspires you?? Do you have a Coach?*

5. *Acid Test Question: What Sales activity or growth opportunities have you been avoiding that would literally change your life?*

Most people say, *"Change is hard"*. I'm here to be a little bit in-your-face and say that *"staying the same is a lot harder"*. So take a deep breath, swallow hard, and work at getting motivated even more! You deserve that much. **NO Excuses.**

Do You Refill Your Tank?

FILL'ER UP... while driving the other day I watched my gas gauge needle slowly move towards empty. Hmmmm... I thought to myself, there is a Daily Sales Tip here. As the day continued, my gas tank level got lower and lower. There was no way to stop it because **in order to get to where I wanted to go, I was burning more fuel.** It reminded me of Dr. John Gray's book ***Men Are from Mars, Women Are from Venus.*** Dr. Gray said that every day we start out with a full tank and then "life happens". The result is that the level of fuel in our tank starts to diminish. This is especially true in the Sales Business. Eventually, if we don't do something about it we are running on empty!

Here is your **ACTION STEP...** commissioned Sales is notorious for "draining the tank". The rejection you receive, the stress of a variable income, the pressure of meeting your goals, and the overall day-to-day uncertainty takes its toll relentlessly! Professional Salespeople need to have a strategy to "refill your tank every day". Here are some ways to do that:

1. *Work on your **Mindset** every day... good books, CDs, inspirational material, affirmations.*

2. *Work on your **Health** every day... frequent exercise, eat wisely, lots of fluids, minimal alcohol.*

3. *Work on your **Associations** every day... surround yourself with positive, supportive, successful people (get rid of the negative ones fast!).*

4. *Work on your **Environment** every day... dress sharp, keep a neat desk, have a sense of urgency, have a clean car*

5. *Work on your **Finances** every day... buy Dave Ramsey's book, "The Total Money Makeover". Do what he says!*

Keep refilling your tank every day. Let's be very clear on this last truism... the need to do so will never go away. Why?... Because as soon as your tank gets low your Sales will start to suffer. You can NEVER let that happen. Make sure that every day you take time to "fill'er up". **NO Excuse.**

Great Insight

WHAT'S IMPORTANT... most Great Salespeople struggle with balancing personal time and their careers. You work very hard to create a great lifestyle for yourself and your family. The problem is sometimes you work so hard that you don't get to enjoy the very thing you're working to support... IE: your personal life!! The good news is you are ambitious, the bad news is it's easy to overdo it. This is ridiculous! Let's do something about it.

Here is your **ACTION STEP...** Here are two great ideas for **balancing business and pleasure:**

1. ***Family...*** *get them to hold you accountable for taking some specific time off. Tell them, "I'm not working next Saturday/Sunday/whatever. What would you like to do?" Here is the cruncher: make an appointment with them, put it in your day timer, turn off your cell phone and enjoy yourself. No more "yeah but"s.*

2. ***Career...*** *eliminate all non-essentials that could easily be classified as "busy work". Practice getting really good at "time blocking"... meaning one task at a time and close the door on all interruptions.*

If having a better life is really important to you then it is **time you put it in your schedule** rather than waiting for it to happen by itself. That hasn't worked so far, and it never will. Give yourself and your family a regular reward. Remember, no on ever went to the grave saying *"I wish I had spent more time at the office"*. **NO Excuses.**

Praise for "All the Right Words"

NEW AGENTS

"I signed a FSBO water front listing by saying exactly what this package told me to say. Thanks Bruce!"

- *Andre Purcell, North Bay, ON*

"When commission cutting "All the Right Words" has given me the confidence to deal with it."

- *Lisa-Marie Wilson, Huntsville, ON*

VETERAN AGENTS

"We listen to the CD's in the car and now have the words just come to us naturally. No more pressure because finally we have "All the Right Words" Thank You, Thank You, Thank You!"

- *Joseph Carlisle and Lisa Boyd, Toronto, ON*

"All the Right Words" gives the framework for my conversations with Buyers and Sellers. Now I don't have to think about what I have to say. The result is I'm a much better listener. Buy this product!"

- *Geoff White, Peterborough, ON*

TOP PRODUCING TEAM

"All the Right Words" has helped my team immeasurably! We did 366 deals last year and we'll do over 400 this year! Thanks Bruce!" - Steven Kuula, Sudbury, ON

Visit www.YouTube/user/BKresults for many more Testimonials

Time Management At Your Fingertips!

"All the Right Time"

"The Complete Package"

1. Get Your Day/Week under Control
2. Innovative Tools That Work
3. 3. Self-Discipline at Your Fingertips!

- A Complete Time Management System resulting from extensive research and 40+ successful years in Sales
- 20 separate components designed to keep you on track
- Too numerous to describe, your package comes with a detailed DVD explaining how to keep "first things first"

Get Your Copy Now At:

www.TimeManagement4You.com

Visit **BruceKeithResults.com**

To Sign Up For Your FREE

"*Weekly Sales Tips*"

About the Author

Bruce Keith
The Results Coach

Bruce's successful Sales Career spans in excess of 40 years. The first 15 years were with IBM Canada Ltd. His duties evolved from direct sales, to marketing, to product management, and ultimately to Sales Training. This excellent Sales and Business training provided a strong platform for his Real Estate career.

He entered the Real Estate profession as a Sales Representative in 1988. He sold real estate for 11 years in central Ontario, in the Newmarket & Aurora area. Very successful, Bruce consistently was a top producer right from the start. He sold in excess of 1000 homes in that time period. In 1999 Bruce and his family moved to Huntsville, Ontario, where he began his Coaching and Seminar career.

Bruce was a Senior Coach for one of the largest coaching organizations in North America for eight years. In 2008 he began operating ***"Bruce Keith Sales Coaching and Seminars"***. The success of his Company speaks for itself. He currently Coaches numerous Salespeople personally and does extensive work with many organizations in both Canada and the USA. His clients include financial advisors, real estate salespeople, personnel recruiting organizations, computer sales organizations, and life insurance salespeople.

An entertaining Speaker, for Bruce return engagements are the norm. His blend of humor, selling skills, and engaging stories ensures that his audiences stay very involved and keeps them coming back. He provides excellent value for his clients by "keeping it simple", providing action oriented techniques, and constantly enhancing the approaches he offers.

As Bruce says,

"***My passion is to help Create the Best Possible Version of You***".

n Calendar Planning Calendar

V - vacation day Red

W = a day Black

E = education Blue

} Year at a Glance Calendar

What's the next step for you?